EASY COMPOSTING

Rodale's **Guides**

Grow-It

EASY COMPOSTING

by Vic Sussman

Rodale Press, Emmaus, Pa.

Printed in the United States of America on recycled paper, containing a high percentage of de-inked fiber.

Art direction by Karen A. Schell

Book design by Joan Peckolick

Illustrations by Jean Seibert

Library of Congress Cataloging in Publication Data

Sussman, Vic S.
    Easy composting.

    (Rodale's grow-it guides)
    Bibliography: p.
    Includes index.
    1. Compost. I. Title. II. Series.
S661.S87   631.8'75   81-19921
ISBN 0-87857-385-2 paperback   AACR2

2 4 6 8 10 9 7 5 3 1 paperback

For Alan M. Pollock, who knows compost when he steps in it.

CONTENTS

INTRODUCTION/**1**
WHAT IS COMPOST?/**2**
HOW TO MAKE COMPOST/**5**
COMPOST ENCLOSURES AND BINS/**36**
HOW AND WHEN TO USE COMPOST/**70**
HOW COMPOST AFFECTS SOIL/**83**
GATHERING COMPOST MATERIALS/**100**
BIBLIOGRAPHY/**133**
INDEX/**134**

INTRODUCTION

C ompost is the foundation of the organic method of gardening. Making compost is the organic gardener's special way of recycling plant and animal wastes that would otherwise be hauled off to landfills or burned in incinerators. Compost returns to the soil organic matter and nutrients that our garden crops take from it as they grow. The processes by which it is made imitate nature's own cycle of life, death and renewal. All the gardener and compost maker does is help speed along the natural process by which organic material is returned to the earth.

Making compost is not difficult, and it is one of the most valuable things a gardener can do. This book explains how and why.

WHAT IS COMPOST?

What's the secret of a successful garden, one overflowing with the riotous colors of mixed flowers, fragrant with herbs, bursting with life-giving vegetables and fruits?

What makes healthy and productive soil—dark, fertile and crumbly—pulse with life?

How can gardeners work in harmony with nature, nourishing and protecting their environment while harvesting its bounty?

Organic gardeners answer these questions with a single word: <u>humus</u>. Walk into any forest and you'll find humus underfoot. Spongy and moist, dark brown or black, humus is of the earth yet something more than mere dirt. Scoop up a handful. Look at it closely. Breathe in its woodsy aroma.

Doesn't look like much, does it? Yet the black granules you hold in your hand are the wellspring of all terrestrial life on our fragile planet. When plants and creatures die, their remains are consumed by myriad soil organisms and reduced to their elemental ingredients.

Humus is thus amorphous, the ebony granules offering no hint of their origins. Animals, insects, plants, bacteria and fungi—whatever lives eventually dies and merges into humus. Grist ground out by the wheel of life, humus embodies the endless cycle of birth-death-renewal.

Yet beyond these spiritual and awesome qualities, humus is fundamental, the lifeblood of productive soil. It makes the difference between an eroded, burned-out tract of land and a flourishing farm, garden or orchard where varied biological and chemical systems thrive in balance.

But natural forces work slowly, taking years and

sometimes centuries to build up even a thin layer of soil-enriching humus. That's why resourceful gardeners and farmers have, since ancient times, turned to composting—a series of steps designed to speed up the natural process of humification.

The only difference between finished compost made by human hands and humus found in the forest is the time it takes to produce it. When you make compost—by whatever process—you're making humus. (Throughout this book we'll use the words compost and humus interchangeably.)

Of course, when you think about it, you can't really make compost—that is, create it—any more than you can germinate a seed or make a tree. These are bio-chemical and mystical events directed by cosmic forces. All we can do is participate in and often initiate them.

That's why making compost is so easy. All you need do is correctly assemble the materials according to some simple principles. You won't have to hire a crew of workers, spend a penny or strain a muscle. Nature will do all the hard work.

In fact, by using the techniques described in this book, some of them developed only in the last few decades, you can turn almost any organic waste into finished compost—rich, black humus—in as little as two weeks! Just follow the easy composting "recipes," put in a few hours of pleasant, healthful work each week, and you'll see kitchen scraps, grass clippings, weeds and even the dust from your vacuum cleaner transformed into valuable compost. Make it by the ton if you have the room or by the bushel if your garden is on an apartment balcony.

But perhaps you're skeptical. You may wonder why organic gardeners have for generations insisted that compost, compost, and more compost is the single most important factor in managing a productive garden of any size. After all, garden shops are filled with boxes, bags and bottles of every imaginable concoction advertised as indispensable to your garden.

How is it possible that something as elemental as the rotted remains of plant and animal wastes can be

By using a method explained in this book, you can construct and manage a compost heap to produce finished compost in two weeks

all things to all soils, a miracle substance you make in your own backyard? Perhaps, if you're new to natural gardening, you may wonder whether this insistence on compost's value is based more on the passionate enthusiasm of organic gardeners than on facts.

Well, consider what modern scientific research has discovered about the value of compost and humus. Agricultural studies around the world have produced a long list of the beneficial effects compost has on the environment. (By the way, there are no bad effects. It's almost impossible to overuse compost or humus. The more you dig into your soil, the better.)

Compost is not only the best soil conditioner but is also an excellent means of recycling wastes

Liberal and regular applications of compost will:

● support and encourage natural soil life, nourishing bacteria, fungi and earthworms, whose activity, in turn, contributes to healthy plant development
● stabilize soil pH, balancing it at a neutral to slightly acid level—the ideal range for most vegetables
● act as a storehouse and natural timed-release dispenser of plant nutrients
● improve the texture and structure of all soils, whether clay or sand, in good condition or bad
● protect soil against drought and erosion
● stop nutrients from being washed out of the soil
● work as a buffer against the buildup of toxins in the soil
● discourage weed growth
● increase the length of the growing season
● return to the land nitrogen, potassium and phosphorus, plus trace elements and naturally occurring substances that are as yet unidentified but that are probably vital to plant and soil health.

All this is possible by using compost, made from materials you might normally throw away.

HOW TO MAKE COMPOST

Before you begin making compost, you should understand the basic principles of how organic matter is converted into humus. Actually, there are only two basic approaches to compost making: fast and slow. Fast piles are hot, with temperatures hitting 160°F at their peak. Slow piles are relatively cool, with temperatures hovering around 110°F and below. All composting methods are simply variations on this theme—either subjecting organic materials to sustained high temperatures or letting them decompose slowly in the cool range.

Both methods have their merits, and both result in valuable humus. Whichever method you choose—and we'll offer guidelines for selecting the best technique for your needs—the basic principles of composting remain the same.

Organic matter: Various microorganisms will convert anything of animal or plant origin into humus if given enough time. Some materials, however, are better suited to the home compost pile than others. (See the chapter Gathering Compost Materials, found later in the book, for more details.) Whatever you choose to compost should be chopped, shredded or split whenever practical to reduce its size and increase its surface area. This allows more room for the agents of decomposition to do their work. Shredding organic matter—stalks, leaves and stems—also speeds rotting by creating entryways for bacteria and fungi, the principal actors in a compost pile.

Microbial life: Like the earth itself, a compost pile is a living community of diverse but interdependent

Coarse, large-particled refuse such as leaves and corn stalks will break down more quickly if you shred them before adding to the compost pile

life forms. Organic matter doesn't merely rot in the abstract. It is consumed and digested by unseen but dynamic organisms that also die in time and are digested.

Think of your compost heap as a thriving factory. The teeming bacteria, fungi, actinomycetes and protozoa are its workers; you are the manager. Provide the minimal requirements for these microscopic employees, and they'll produce rich humus unceasingly. And all they need is the correct blend of organic matter, air, moisture and temperature.

Air: The two types of composting—fast and slow—depend on different microorganisms with differing requirements for air. Slow decomposition, in fact, needs no oxygen whatever. Its microbes work under anaerobic, or airless, conditions. Materials rotted anaerobically can break down in closed vessels like drums and tanks or sealed under plastic sheeting.

Plenty of air circulation is essential when making compost by the quick method

Fast composting, however, demands air, plenty of it, regularly recirculated by turning or fluffing the materials. If you start a fast compost pile but neglect air circulation, or if the pile becomes waterlogged, squeezing the oxygen out, the aerobic process will change. The aerobes will consume all the available oxygen, then die off. Anaerobes will become dominant, and the composting process will take considerably longer. Time doesn't matter to a microbe, but it may to you.

Something else that may matter is the physical difference between anaerobic and aerobic decomposition. Aerobic piles have no unpleasant odors. The rotting materials take on the aroma of the forest floor or mushrooms. An anaerobic heap, however, can give off a considerable stink, particularly if its ingredients include kitchen scraps.

Gardeners have devised all kinds of systems to feed air to the inner depths of a compost pile. Some use perforated plastic pipes jammed into the heap vertically and horizontally. Others use branches, strips of scrap lumber or twisted bundles of brush in the same manner. Another method involves building the pile over crisscross sunflower stalks, which rot in time, leaving air channels within the pile. And some composters claim success with heaps built over heavy-duty screen or grates. Air is supposed to enter the heap from below.

But none of these methods conducts large amounts of air to all parts of the heap. Only one technique accomplishes that, and it is one that many gardeners prefer to avoid: turning or chopping the pile every three or four days. This is either hard work or good exercise, depending on how you look at it, but it's the most effective way to maintain a hot, fast-acting, aerobic compost pile.

It's also possible to construct heaps—using the classic Indore method—that start out aerobic and slowly become anaerobic without developing bad odors or slime. Still, providing adequate air to decomposing materials, especially in the early stages, is important in the building of efficient, inoffensive compost piles.

Moisture: A pile of excessively wet organic matter—garbage or manure, for example—will decay anaerobically. Because all the pores in the material are filled with water instead of oxygen, the decay bacteria will work slowly at a low temperature while producing a stench. This is bearable if you compost your wastes in a covered pit, underground or in a sealed tank, but for most people a nonputrid heap will be most welcome.

Balancing a heap's need for moisture is often the key to successful aerobic composting. A pile that is too wet will compact and produce slime, while one that's too dry will just sit there, decomposing at a glacial pace.

All materials in a compost pile should be about as damp as a wrung-out sponge. You can achieve this by layering wet and dry matter. Mix garbage with hay or dry leaves; fresh cow or horse manure with straw or other bedding; green, wet grass clippings with dead leaves. And keep your garden hose or sprinkling can handy. Some materials, such as hay, straw, dead leaves and sawdust, shed water easily or merely absorb it into their surface. Sprinkle these until the ingredients glisten, then stir them up to be sure the moisture has been distributed throughout the fibers.

If you're making fast, high heat compost—turning the pile every three days—you may have to add water again after the first turning. This is the time you'll note the heap's rising temperature. If there's no heat but everything else is correct (adequate nitrogen and air), the

A good guide to use in gauging how wet compost materials should be is to make them as damp as a wrung-out sponge

problem is probably an imbalance in the moisture content. If the materials seem too dry, spray or sprinkle each layer as you pull the pile apart for turning.

If the pile is too wet—you'll realize this from the lack of heat, bad odors and water running off in rivulets —mix in more absorbent matter until all the materials are equally damp.

Nitrogen: Many gardeners pile up prunings, leaves and culled weeds in an out-of-the-way spot. Years pass before these brush piles decay into usable humus. But, properly managed, the same materials could be turned into finished compost in less than a month, or a year at most. What's the secret? Adequate air and moisture are important, as we've seen, but the key to rapid, hot composting is nitrogen.

Like all living creatures, the microbes at work in a compost heap need a balanced diet in order to survive and reproduce. Like us, they need carbon (carbo-

Like all living creatures, the microbes at work in a compost heap need a balanced diet in order to survive and reproduce. Like us, they need carbon (carbo-hydrates) and nitrogen (protein) for optimum energy production and tissue maintenance. Scientists call this and moisture, the well-nourished aerobic organisms will quickly multiply and feed on the assembled plant and animal matter. Their activity will produce the high temperatures characteristic of a rapidly decaying compost pile.

But if the C/N ratio is off because of excess carbon —at 100 to 1, for instance—the pile won't heat up. Decomposition, as in the untended brush pile, will merely plod along. Of course, there's no way the C/N ratio of your compost heap can be precisely measured without sophisticated laboratory equipment. But, fortunately, that's not necessary. You can easily learn to use your eyes, nose and experience to judge when a pile's C/N balance is correct.

All organic matter contains carbon and nitrogen, but in varying amounts. A few materials, such as good quality hay and soybean stalks, fall naturally into that ideal 25 or 30 to 1 ratio, but most materials are either high or low in carbon or nitrogen and must be blended. If your mixture contains too much carbon,

The best ratio of carboniferous to nitrogen-containing materials for a compost heap is about 25 to 1

the microbes will consume all the available nitrogen and then quit, leaving the leftover carboniferous matter unrotted and the pile well below pasteurizing temperatures. If the heap contains too much nitrogen, however, the excess will be thrown off by the microbes as ammonia gas. You'll have no trouble noticing this characteristic odor.

To balance the C/N ratio of your compostables, start by consulting the chart titled Carbon/Nitrogen Ratios of Various Organic Materials. Note that you can mix ingredients to average out to the ideal ratio.

CARBON/NITROGEN RATIOS OF VARIOUS ORGANIC MATERIALS

Alfalfa	13 to 1	Mature sweet clover	23 to 1
Alfalfa hay	12 to 1	Oat straw	80 to 1
Cornstalks	60 to 1	Paper	170 to 1
Food wastes (table scraps)	15 to 1	Rotted manure	20 to 1
Fruit wastes	35 to 1	Sawdust	500 to 1
Grass clippings	19 to 1	Sewage sludge: activated	6 to 1
Green sweet clover	16 to 1	Sewage sludge: digested	16 to 1
Humus	10 to 1	Straw	80 to 1
Leaves a range of 80 to 1–40 to 1		Sugar cane residues	50 to 1
Legume-grass hay	25 to 1	Wood	700 to 1

For example, one part fruit wastes (such as apple pomace left over after making cider) to two parts grass clippings or manure would balance out at 25 to 1. A mixture of kitchen scraps, grass clippings, rotted manure and dead leaves would also approach the ideal, as would one part oat straw to one part manure, or equal parts of hay, grass and cornstalks. Be sure to mix all the ingredients by weight, not volume. The chart will help you work out your own combinations according to the materials you have on hand.

But remember that the chart is just a guide. You'll soon learn to judge the carbon and nitrogen content of materials by their source and appearance. For example, most animal wastes, such as manure, hair, feathers and urine, are high in nitrogen. Fresh green

Kitchen scraps are usually a good source of wet, nitrogen-rich compost materials

plant matter, coffee grounds and seed meals, such as soybean and cottonseed meals, are also nitrogenous.

Carboniferous matter is usually brittle, old and dark brown. Dried plant stalks, dead leaves, bark and other wood wastes are high in carbon and will break down slowly unless you add ample nitrogen. (Note also that you cannot use finished compost to activate a new pile, because humus has a C/N ratio of 10 to 1.)

Household garbage is an unusually good source of compostable materials rich in nitrogen and trace minerals. Kitchen scraps can be composted rapidly and odorlessly when mixed with absorbent matter like leaves, hay or dry grass clippings.

Achieving the correct carbon/nitrogen balance is crucial if you want a fast, hot compost pile that will yield black humus in less than a month. But don't let the numbers throw you; they're just a guide that you can use until you've made a few successful batches. Actually, your compost pile will tell you when the C/N ratio is correct. If all the materials are moist but not wet and the pile still doesn't heat up to 110° to 120°F within 48 hours, you probably need more nitrogen. On the other hand, if the pile heats up but has a strong odor of ammonia, you've added too much nitrogen. You needn't correct this. Just use it as a reminder to add a little less nitrogenous matter in your next heap, assuming it contains similar materials.

In general, it's wise for a beginning composter to mix in lots of nitrogen-rich matter in your first several compost heaps. You'll lose some nitrogen to the atmosphere, but you'll insure that the pile develops sufficient heat for rapid decomposition.

And by the way, if you're a city or suburban gardener, you'll be happy to see that it's not absolutely necessary to have manure for an efficient compost pile. True, manure is a concentrated source of nitrogen and is convenient to use. But city dwellers often have trouble getting it at low or no cost and in sufficient amounts, not to mention bringing it home without alarming the neighbors.

The C/N chart and practical experience demonstrate that even the most urban of gardeners can produce ample humus with nothing more than castoffs—dead leaves, grass clippings and kitchen scraps.

Composting Methods

What's the best way to make compost? No one can answer that question but you. The best method is the one that most effectively serves your needs as a gardener. You must, when choosing a composting technique, take several factors into account. How much gardening area do you have? How much compost will you need? How much time will you have to make compost? What kinds and amounts of organic materials are available to you?

Of course, all compost, no matter how it's produced, ends up as humus—the most valuable stuff you can add to your soil. So any composting technique that enables you to enrich your land regularly (even if you're gardening in containers) is worthwhile. But each method has certain characteristics that may or may not fit your needs. Let's begin with a classic composting technique.

Choose among the many methods and structures for composting according to how much compost you need and the kinds of materials you can get easily

The Indore Method: This method was named after the area in India where it was first developed by Sir Albert Howard, a British agronomist. Howard lived in India from 1905 to 1934, where he worked to improve depleted soils and unproductive farming methods.

Generally considered the father of the organic method, Howard perceived that the path to optimal soil fertility was through the application of abundant humus. The systematic method of composting he developed used plant wastes and animal manure piled in layers with infrequent but regular turnings.

The Indore method develops some heat at the outset, but it's primarily a slow-working, anaerobic heap free of the usual odors found in haphazardly made anaerobic piles. This method may suit you if you have plenty of land, don't mind waiting until the materials slowly break down, and prefer to turn the pile as little as possible. Indore heaps usually sit for a minimum of three months in mild weather, sometimes longer, depending on the type and condition of the materials in the pile.

The minimum pile size should be 3 feet square by 3 to 5 feet high. (Howard's basic heaps were 6 feet wide, 3 to 5 feet high and 10 to 30 feet in length.) You may either use a bin or simply mark off the

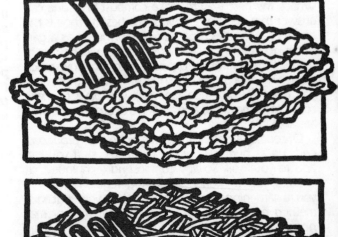

INDORE COMPOST HEAP: First, spread a 6-inch layer of plant debris as the base of the pile. Next, add a 2-inch layer of manure and bedding. Cover the first two layers with a thin layer (⅛ inch) of

dimensions of the pile on the ground, scratching the boundaries with a spade.

Spread out a 6-inch-deep layer of plant wastes within the boundary marks of the pile. This forms the base of your pile. Use hay, straw, sawdust, leaves, grass clippings, corncobs or cornstalks, garbage or wood chips.

Next, add a 2-inch layer of manure and bedding atop the base.

Sprinkle a thin (⅛-inch) layer of topsoil over this. (Urine-impregnated soil from a barnyard or stable is especially valuable.)

Next, spread atop this any various soil amendments —granite dust, phosphate rock, greensand or wood

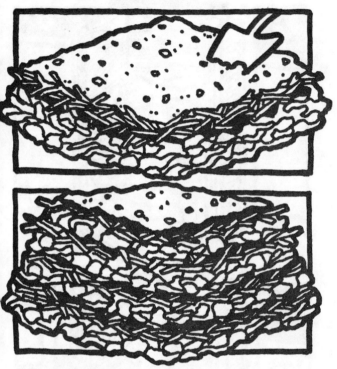

soil; rock powders and soil amendments can be added at this time. Repeat layers until the pile is 4 feet high. The finished pile should be at least 3 feet square by 3 to 4 feet high.

ashes. These add minerals to the finished compost and will be broken down by the decaying process into forms more available to plant roots.

Continue building these alternating layers of plant wastes, manure and soil until the pile stands 3 to 4 feet tall, making sure all ingredients are sufficiently moist. Add water by sprinkling or spraying, if necessary. If you plan to let the pile sit unturned you may also want to add vertical and horizontal sticks or pipes (metal or plastic) as you build the layers. These rods will help bring air into more of the pile, although they won't create total aeration.

The pile should show some evidence of heating within two days after the initial building. If you detect

An Indore-type heap must be 3 to 4 feet tall; a lower pile won't have sufficient volume, and a higher pile will be hard to turn

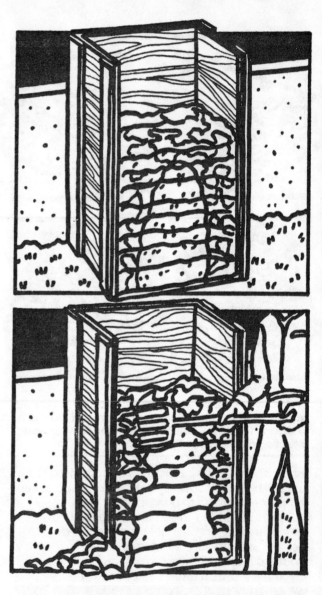

no heat (temperatures should rise to at least 110°F), check the moisture and nitrogen content, adding whichever is appropriate. You'll have to tear the pile apart to do this, of course, another reason to supply plenty of moisture and nitrogen right from the start.

Turn the pile with a pitchfork three weeks from the day you started it, removing any aerating sticks or

TURNING THE COMPOST HEAP: *Remove the compost from the bin with a pitchfork, keeping the material from the outside of the pile separate from the material from the inside (left). Put the compost back into the bin with the compost originally on the outside now in the middle and the compost taken from the middle now on the outside of the pile (above).*

pipes as you work. This turning will mix the separate layers, incorporating all of the materials into a homogenized mass. But keep track of how you dismantle the heap. When you rebuild the pile you'll want to put the ingredients that were on the outside of the heap into its interior and vice versa. The object is to insure that all materials spend some time in the pile's interior, where composting temperatures are the highest and microbial activity is the most active. You may also have to add water during this first turning.

The second turning comes three weeks later. You should notice higher temperatures at this point, 130° to 150°F, though these will decline as the decomposition process continues.

The contents will be finished decaying in about three to six months from when they were first assembled. This time period varies, however, depending on how often the pile was turned and what kinds of materials were used. Even after six months some ingredients like matted leaves and fibrous stalks may remain relatively undecayed. Use these to start your next pile.

There's nothing sacred about the schedule of turnings. You may turn as suggested above or make the first turning at 6 weeks, the second at 12 weeks. You may also turn the pile more frequently (in which case the decomposition will be speeded up) or not at all. Many gardeners prefer this last course, avoiding the labor of forking a ton or more of organic matter from one place to another.

If you don't want to turn the heap, cover it with sod or plastic to keep odors in and flies out

If you choose to do no turning, build the pile as suggested, but cover it at the finish with inverted mats of sod or a sheet of black plastic. If you use plastic, be sure to weight or peg it down securely so it is not blown away by the wind. These coverings will cause the heap to operate anaerobically, but because you've layered wet and dry materials, you should have no problem with escaping odors or flies. An unturned pile will take at least a year to decompose thoroughly.

The main advantages of the Indore and similar slow composting methods are that they can accommodate large amounts of organic matter while making minimal physical demands on the composter. Once you've constructed a heap you can let nature do all the work.

The disadvantages of slow composting, however, are that the piles take up space for six months or more and fail to produce sustained pasteurizing temperatures throughout the pile. This means that weed seeds and some pathogens survive the composting process.

Still, if you have a large lot, a substantial amount of organic matter and a supply of finished compost to use while you wait for the heap to decay, and if you dislike the work of regularly turning a pile, the classic Indore method might be right for you.

Trenching or Compostholing: These are both fancy names for burying garbage and other organic matter, a basic but valuable means of soil building. When you bury organic wastes, you're creating an underground compost pile. Decomposition will be anaerobic and relatively slow, but it will also be odorless, invisible and convenient.

There are several approaches to trenching, but they all share a number of characteristics. First of all, the materials should have 4 to 6 inches of dirt covering them; any less when burying kitchen scraps is an invitation to scavengers. Second, bury all materials in

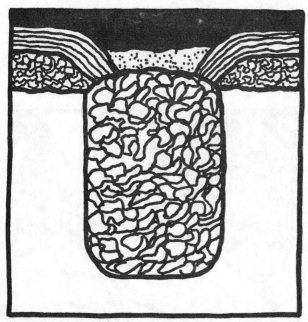

HOW TO TRENCH: *Dig a trench 12 inches deep and 12 to 18 inches wide. Fill with any kind of organic matter and cover with soil. These trenches that house underground mulch can be dug into garden paths or in fallow garden areas that will be used for planting the following season.*

garden areas that will be left fallow for a year. You cannot plant or transplant directly over freshly buried wastes without risking a nitrogen deficiency in your crops. (As fresh organic matter decomposes, it uses soil nitrogen, temporarily depriving the immediate area and nearby plants of this crucial element.)

To use the trenching method, dig trenches 12 inches deep and 12 to 18 inches wide. Fill them with any type of organic matter, and cover with dirt. You may

17

When burying kitchen scraps in a garden trench, dig them in deep enough so scavenging animals won't find them

pile mulch over this if you wish. These trenches may be dug into garden paths that will be used as planting sites the following year. You may also dig trenches in unused sections of the garden or in areas you plan to turn into garden spaces in the future. Gardeners working in raised beds can trench down the center of the bed in fall or add raw materials as they rebuild the beds, double-digging at summer's end.

For compostholing, use a clamshell posthole digger to make 12-inch-deep holes in strategic spots — between rows, in movable paths (as described above) or near crops that will stay in one place all season (parsnips,

COMPOSTHOLING: *Dig 12-inch-deep holes in strategic spots in the garden with a clamshell posthole digger. Fill the holes with plant debris or kitchen scraps, and finish off with a layer of good topsoil.*

tomatoes and peppers, for example). Dig several holes ahead of time so you'll always have a place to recycle each day's kitchen scraps.

The disadvantages of trenching and compostholing are that they involve digging, which is heavier work in some cases than turning a compost heap; that they demand some extra garden planning; and that they present the risk of temporary nitrogen loss in the soil. (Don't place trenches or garbage-filled holes too close to growing plants; keep a safety margin of about 12 to 18 inches.) And, while convenient, neither trenching nor compostholing will produce compost that can be used as mulch, sidedressing, or potting soil. However, the process is certainly simple, involving no concern for the carbon/nitrogen ratio of materials, no turning or inspection and no use of valuable surface area. Compost gets made on the spot right in the garden, so you also save the work of hauling humus back and forth.

Burying scraps, manure and other materials can, based on my own experience, rapidly improve poor soil. The technique builds deep deposits of humus right into the growing area while progressively loosening and fracturing the soil. Heavy clay in particular can be dramatically improved by regular trenching and compostholing.

Pit Composting: This is another anaerobic method. Unlike trenching, however, the pit involved is larger and generally permanent. You can hopscotch trenches around the garden, but a pit should be located in an out-of-the-way but convenient area—near the kitchen or barn, perhaps, depending on what you intend to compost.

Pit composting is slow and requires a permanent space, but it requires no work after the pit is dug and filled

Pit composting makes considerable use of naturally occurring earthworms and soil bacteria to effect decomposition. No turning or layering of materials is necessary, although much heavy digging must be done during the initial excavation of the pit. Decomposition is lengthy and uneven, especially if large amounts of garbage are used. It's not unusual to find pockets of undigested, slimy wastes when digging into compost pits filled with what appears to be fully decomposed matter.

The best approach is to have two pits or some other composting arrangement in addition to a working pit.

That way you can fill the second pit or bin while the original pit's contents move toward total decomposition.

Unlike trenching, pit composting will produce humus for mulch and sidedressing, though none of the material will have achieved pasteurizing temperatures.

Full instructions for building and maintaining a compost pit are given in the next chapter, Compost Enclosures and Bins.

Sheet Composting: This is the least complicated of all soil-building methods. It's also the most natural initially in that it mimics nature's pattern of depositing organic material directly on the soil surface. Compostables are simply scattered or piled atop the garden area or beneath the drip line of trees.

But sheet composting may take two forms. The scattered materials — hay, plant residues or manure — may be tilled under 4 to 12 inches, where they will rot slowly, breaking down through the activity of worms and microorganisms. Or the organic matter may be left on the surface as a permanent mulch, decaying even more slowly.

Sheet composting using tillage is more useful on the farm than in the home garden because it usually involves tying up large tracts of land, often delaying or postponing their planting in favor of soil building. But gardeners with large plots can spread manure heavily in the fall or early spring, tilling it under immediately so as to minimize nutrient loss by leaching. If fresh manure or green matter is tilled under in spring, however, the materials must be thoroughly incorporated no less than a month before planting.

Sheet composting is best used for very large garden plots or for farm fields

Sheet composting using fresh organic matter always presents the risk of creating temporary but troublesome nitrogen deficiencies as the materials decay. The safest method is to use alternate plots, sheet composting and gardening them in rotation. Few home gardeners have the luxury of owning so much land, however.

If you do have a plot you wish to sheet-compost, try this elaborate but effective method. First mow down all surface vegetation. Then, spread a layer of organic matter evenly over the area. This may be hay, manure and bedding, corncobs, silage or virtually any other organic matter. Spread the materials evenly. Then broadcast any or all of several soil amendments— phosphate rock, greensand, granular seaweed or granite dust. (Wear a suitable dust mask when spreading these powders.) Use a tiller or spade to turn under all materials to a depth of at least 4 inches. Let everything rot thoroughly before seeding or transplanting into the plot. This process usually takes several months or more, depending on weather conditions and the kinds of materials tilled under.

Rock dusts are safe and effective amendments to use in this manner. They're slow acting and won't burn or poison plants as can quick-acting synthetic fertilizers. Application rates vary according to the mineral content of your soil, but a general guide for using rock dusts would be to apply about 5 to 10 pounds per 100 square feet of growing area. A similar application rate may be used for granular seaweed.

Sheet composting by scattering materials does have some obvious disadvantages. The incorporation of raw organic matter close to planting time risks nitrogen lockup; no pasteurized compost suitable for use as potting soil or sidedressing will be available; the organic matter must be mechanically turned under by a tiller or plow or worked in with a spade. In addition, weed seeds and plant pathogens are left unscathed by the cool anaerobic temperatures when the material breaks down.

On the other hand, the method has the decided advantage of simplicity. Materials are dumped on and worked in, and they need no tending or inspection. There are other advantages, too: huge amounts of organic matter may be directly and quickly incorporated into the soil; the decomposition process warms the soil and releases carbon dioxide directly to the root zone; the local soil organisms are nourished firsthand instead of getting materials already digested by the denizens of the compost pile; and fresh manure, usually available in large quantities at low cost, is—if unleached by rain— richer in soluble nitrogen and potash than the humus found in a traditional compost heap.

Permanent Mulch: This variation on sheet composting has helped many gardeners to improve their soil while

A deep layer of permanent mulch eliminates any need for weeding or watering the garden, and it adds organic matter to the soil very slowly

SHEET COMPOSTING: *Remove all surface vegetation with a scythe (top left). Spread organic matter evenly over the area and broadcast soil amendments over the plot (bottom left). Turn under all material to a depth of at least 4 inches (above). Leave it to rot several months before planting.*

combating weeds and drought. Popularized by the late Ruth Stout as the "no-work system," the permanent mulch method usually employs heavy annual applications of hay, straw or dead leaves. These materials are piled on, allowed to settle, then constantly added to until the mulch is at least 6 inches thick.

Decomposition takes place slowly as earthworms drag bits of organic matter downward and soil bacteria work on the material in contact with the earth. High-nitrogen supplements like cottonseed or soy meal may also be added during the season to boost plant growth.

The soil under the mulch, while never tilled or spaded, will become progressively loose and humusy over the years due to the continual buildup of organic matter and the activity of worms.

PERMANENTLY MULCHED GARDEN: *A layer of hay or straw at least 6 inches deep provides a permanent mulch that serves to control weeds and combat drought while slowly enriching the soil.*

To plant in a permanently mulched garden, pull the mulch aside in early spring to allow the soil to warm. Then seed or transplant as usual, pulling the mulch back around the plant stems as growth proceeds.

A permanent mulch enriches the soil slowly, conserves moisture, discourages weed growth by limiting light and moderates soil temperatures. And as Ruth Stout was fond of pointing out, a permanent mulch releases the gardener forevermore from hoeing, tilling and digging.

But the system does have its drawbacks. You'll have to spend a lot of time and money rounding up those mulch materials unless you have a source of free materials. Even spoiled hay is no longer cheap. And covering your entire plot with organic matter means you'll be mulching unproductive areas like paths as well as growing areas. In a traditional garden, paths may amount to 40 percent of the total area.

A permanently mulched garden may therefore force you to grow crops in rows, using more space to grow less food than in an raised-bed intensive garden or even a traditional garden with wide and closely spaced rows. But if your soil is poor in organic content, and if you have access to considerable amounts of mulch materials and a relatively large garden area, then the no-work permanent mulch garden may be the method for you.

The preceding methods—the classic Indore heap, trenching, compostholing, pit composting, sheet composting and permanent mulches are all examples of slow, low-heat decomposition. They will yield humus in large amounts but only over a relatively long period of time. However, time is often something gardeners don't have in great supply, so you may want to make compost more rapidly.

Fast Composting

The techniques for making fast, hot compost evolved from research originally done at the Sanitary Engineering Department of the University of California at Berkeley. This work, which took place in the early 1950s, was directed by waste treatment expert and research biologist Dr. Clarence G. Golueke. The object was to study the practicality of using composting techniques to recycle municipal wastes.

Although the studies investigated composting on a grand scale, they also gave birth to a methodology for rapid composting that is ideally suited to the gardener and small farmer. Golueke showed that properly balanced organic matter could be turned into finished compost in just 12 days! (He used garden debris, kitchen scraps and dead leaves in one experiment.)

Fast composting demands more work but produces results more quickly than any other method

This technique obviously demands more attention and effort than the slow-acting Indore heap, but the principles involved are quite simple:

● The raw materials must have a correctly balanced carbon/nitrogen ratio. Four parts plant matter to one part manure, if available, would be a rough guide.

● The greater the variety of materials used, the more effective the overall composting process. Microorganisms like a varied diet.

• The working pile should be built all at once, not over several days or weeks. This is to conserve the nitrogen content in the materials. If you cannot build the pile at once, keep accumulating ingredients under cover, especially protected against rain.

• While not an absolute necessity, a bin or enclosure should be used for best results. A frame of some type will allow the pile to be built taller, providing more mass. A bin will also stop the materials from "wandering" as you turn the pile while protecting against drying winds and scavengers.

• The minimum pile size is a cubic yard, 3 by 3 by 3 feet tall. But this is the completed size. Organic matter settles after piling, losing almost half its original height.

CORRECT PILE DIMENSIONS FOR FAST COMPOST-ING: *For best and fastest results, the size of the finished compost pile should be at least 3 feet square by 3 feet high, which means you should start with a pile at least 4 feet high. This allows enough mass for the pile to heat up to optimum temperatures for fast decomposition.*

It's best to build a heap at least 4 feet tall to start. This minimum size is necessary to provide mass enough to heat up, plus some self-insulating qualities. If your climate is cool, however, or if you're starting to compost in late fall, the minimum pile size should be even larger to compensate for the lower air temperatures.

• Materials may be layered initially as in the Indore method to insure the proper proportioning of matter according to its moisture content and carbon content, or they may be thoroughly mixed.

• For fastest decomposition, the heap must be aerated by turning every second or third day from the day the pile was first made. Turning the pile at longer intervals extends the composting process. Turning the heap more often—every day—may speed decay somewhat, but more than one turning daily is unnecessary.

• All materials to be composted should be reduced in size before they are added to the pile. The smaller the particle size involved, the more rapid the decomposition process.

This last line may make you think you'll need a power shredder, but an adequate job can be done using simple hand tools. The key is to chop all coarse materials before and during the composting. Stalks and stems can be quickly reduced to 6-inch chunks with a machete or hachet. Dead leaves, matted animal bedding and hay and straw clumps can be chopped apart with a 10-pound mattock or grubbing hoe. (A regular garden hoe is too light for this job and will break.) You can also run your lawn mower over piles of matted leaves, directing the stream of particles against a wall or fence.

Even after this preparation, however, the ingredients you're using may continue to pack down in the pile. Again, use the mattock or grubbing hoe to chop the pile apart every second or third day. Don't simply use a pitchfork to flip the stuff from one place to another. The more you're able to reduce the particle size and aerate the mass, the faster you'll have humus instead of raw materials.

A reasonable turning schedule for finished compost in two weeks would be as follows, counting from the day you made the heap: turn on the second, fourth, seventh and tenth days.

Materials for a fast compost heap must be shredded or chopped, but don't use your garden hoe for the job—it's too lightweight

TESTING TEMPERATURES: *If you don't have a meat or candy thermometer, an iron pipe placed in the middle of your compost pile can tell you whether your pile is getting hot enough. Insert an iron pipe into the core of the pile and leave it there for ten minutes. If the pipe is too hot to touch, then the pile is working well.*

Let your thermometer guide you until you're able to judge from experience alone. You can measure the temperature of the pile by sticking a deep-fat or nursery thermometer into the center of the pile. Or, if you don't have this kind of thermometer on hand, place an iron pipe down into the core of the pile, wait 10 minutes, and if the pipe is too hot to touch, you'll know the pile has heated up sufficiently. The pile should heat to 110° to 120°F by the second or third day, to 130° to 160°F (or above, in some instances) by the fourth or fifth day, and should then hold in that range as the decomposition process works toward a peak. The temperature will gradually decline after that (usually around the tenth day, depending on your turning schedule), cooling to about 110°F. The pile is done when further turnings do not raise the temperature beyond 110°F.

The materials can be aged still further, but they can be safely used in the garden anytime after their temperature settles down to 110°F or below.

Turning and chopping a pile on this schedule is good cardiovascular exercise, which is a fancy way of saying hard work. A pile 3 by 3 by 8 feet long will take about 45 minutes to chop and turn the first few times; it will take somewhat less time as the material thoroughly rots. But this physical effort and the systematic attention that must be paid to making hot, fast compost are its only drawbacks. The benefits are more numerous.

Dr. Golueke says that with rapid, hot composting "not only are the high temperatures reached, they persist for days, ensuring complete pasteurization." University of California researchers found that compost naturally "cooking" at 131°F kills all but the most hardy disease organisms (plant and human) and fly larvae in the first 24 to 48 hours.

The high temperatures reached in a fast compost pile kill weed seeds and pathogens, in effect pasteurizing the compost

And high heat, says Golueke, isn't the only factor in bumping off pathogens. Fungi and actinomycetes (a type of bacteria) in the pile produce natural antibiotic substances during the high heat stages; these are important for healthy soil and plant life.

Temperatures from 120°F to 160°F also destroy weed seeds, a significant advantage of hot composting over slow or sheet composting methods. Shoveling on manure also shovels on all the weed seeds that come through an animal's intestines intact. Those frequent turnings while making hot compost guarantee that weed seeds have the life fried out of them.

Hot compost is a sign of highly active microbial activity. Thermophilic bacteria (those that live at 113° to 158°F) multiply more rapidly than their mesophilic relatives (operating up to 104°F) and are capable of greater enzymatic activity. Dr. W. D. Bellamy, a Cornell University microbiologist, says that "the bacteria that carry out the chemical reactions in a compost pile go faster at high temperatures than they do at low temperatures. What takes many months at low temperatures may take only a few weeks at high."

Nor will you have to worry about offensive odors when making fast compost. Kitchen scraps added to the core of a hot pile will be digested in days. (You must chop up large scraps like apples, whole potatoes, rotten oranges, stalks and the like before adding them.) Keep all food scraps mixed well into the interior of the pile, and you'll have no problem with scavengers or flies,

The humic acids produced in a hot compost heap hold trace elements in a form that can be used by plant roots

since there will be no odors to attract them.

When you first throw mixed compostable materials together, their pH levels may range widely from acid to alkaline. But hot composting rapidly balances out these variations. During the thermophilic stage (113° to 158°F) the pile's overall pH will drop 4.5 to 5.0. Once the temperature hits a peak above 130°F, the pH will become more alkaline, from 7.5 to 8.5. And when the decay process is finished, the compost's pH will range from neutral to slightly alkaline—the correct range for most vegetables.

Hot compost also produces abundant humic acids. These are natural chelating composts that absorb the ions of trace minerals—copper, iron, manganese and zinc—holding them in an available form until plants can take them up in solution. Without the activity of humic acids, these nutrients would remain chemically bound in forms useless to plants.

The production of humic acids may be hot compost's most important benefit. These substances actually act like food storehouses, holding various elements until the soil warms up and plant growth increases. Then soil fungi and bacteria attack the chelates, freeing their stored nutrients.

Russian researchers have reported that humic acids and their derivatives promote the uptake of nutrients by increasing the permeability of plant membranes. And yet another study showed that humic acids not only encourage soil aggregation but also increase the permanence of the crumbs already formed. (More about this topic will be covered in the chapter How Compost Affects Soil, found later in the book.)

Fast, hot composting obviously has significant benefits. The technique can also be a blessing if you're a city or suburban gardener working a small plot with neighbors close by. You probably don't have the room for a large, slow-working Indore pile, nor can you wait a year or more between batches of finished compost. By using rapid composting you can make several loads of humus each season using stuff you find right in your own neighborhood, much of it (grass clippings and leaves) left conveniently bagged on the curb.

Making just three compost piles a season (each heap a cubic yard, 3 by 3 by 3 feet) between early spring and fall would supply you with roughly 1,500 pounds of humus. That's enough to cover three 5 by 20-foot beds with 3 inches of compost!

Making Compost in an Apartment

Apartment dwellers can make compost. The method you use and the amount of humus you produce depend on your living arrangements. Do you have a garden apartment with a patio or a small yard? Or perhaps you have a rooftop garden. If so, you can probably fit in a permanent 3 by 3 by 4-foot bin (see the next chapter, Compost Enclosures and Bins, for construction details).

But those readers who live in more confined spaces can also convert kitchen scraps into compost—right in the kitchen. For this simple but effective method you need to obtain several 5-gallon plastic buckets with lids. They can be garbage or diaper pails or discarded drywall compound cans. Stay with the 5-gallon size; anything much larger will be hard to lift when full of humus. All pails should have bailing handles for easier moving.

Fill one pail with ordinary dirt, not sterilized potting soil, pasteurized topsoil, or the peat humus sold in garden shops. You want soil alive with microorganisms. Dig some out of a friend's garden or a patch of woods. Or call your local park service for permission to dig on public land.

Set the empty and dirt-filled buckets side by side in a spot convenient to your kitchen. A floor-level cupboard or closet will do, or you can put the pails under a table. You'll also need a trowel.

The secret of apartment composting is to use the scraps immediately, reducing their bulk by shredding or chopping them. A sharp knife or cleaver is fine for this purpose, but a blender or food processor is ideal; it will finish the job in seconds, reducing even fibrous stalks to a slurry. Scraps cut up with a knife will work just as well, but they will take longer to compost.

Take each day's accumulation of scraps—or each meal's, if you prefer—and whiz them into a semiliquid, adding a little water if needed. Don't use bones, meat or fish scraps because they take too long to break down and may produce odors. Blend everything else, though—eggshells, fruit and vegetable scraps, coffee

The key to making compost successfully indoors is to use the suitable kitchen scraps at once, before they begin to develop odors

ROOFTOP COMPOST: *For those who garden in rooftop gardens, a compost bin fits well in an inconspicuous corner, cleverly hidden by a potted tree.*

and tea grounds. Pour this brew into the empty bucket, covering the puree with a 1-inch layer of dirt. Add fresh materials at least once a day, covering the slurry every

COMPOSTING BUCKETS IDEAL FOR APARTMENT DWELLERS: *Apartment dwellers can convert all their kitchen scraps into excellent compost in 5-gallon buckets neatly tucked away in the kitchen or on a terrace.*

time with a layer of dirt. Stir the contents daily with the trowel or a stick to incorporate plenty of oxygen. (This stirring is the equivalent of turning a full-size heap with a pitchfork.)

The key to success with this method is to always use <u>fresh</u> kitchen scraps. Don't let them sit overnight, or they'll begin developing odors and slime and become unpleasant to work with. Fresh scraps are merely unused food. Old scraps are garbage. Using kitchen wastes as you produce them, covering them with microbially active soil and stirring them occasionally means you'll have no problem with odors or flies (which are attracted by odors).

This composting method is aerobic, but the mix won't develop any significant heat. Follow the routine above to keep the aerobes healthy, making sure the slurry-dirt mix is always moist and never waterlogged or starved for oxygen. If you choose to keep the can covered to discourage curious cats and small children, put the lid on loosely, or punch it full of holes before snapping it on.

Start filling another compost bucket when your first one is two-thirds full. Set the full pail aside while the second one is filling, but keep stirring the first bucket occasionally, checking on the progress of humification. The compost should be finished in about two weeks. Sift through it. You should no longer be able to tell what the original scraps were composed of (except for some particles of eggshell, perhaps). The soil should look crumbly and humusy. Feed it to your house plants, put it in your window boxes or carry it in a bucket to your community garden plot.

Apartment composting is easy, practical and productive while keeping you in touch with the natural world. Besides helping you turn your wastes into a resource, the method described is an excellent school project for children.

Choosing the Right Method

Choosing between these methods—whether fast or slow composting—isn't easy unless you live in an apartment with few options to begin with. Each method has its drawbacks and advantages. Of course, the very best way to improve and maintain your soil is to use two or three of the major composting methods combined in an organized program. This assumes that you have the space, sufficient organic matter and plenty of time. Here is an example of an excellent year-around composting schedule:

Fall: Start by sheet composting, working plenty of organic matter into the top few inches of the garden. Leave the ground surface rough so freezing and thawing can mellow the soil and destroy exposed insect eggs and larvae. At about the same time, at least a month before the first hard freeze, begin a fast-working compost pile. When the compost is finished in two or three weeks, remove some of it for use as potting soil next spring. Cover the rest of the compost so rain doesn't leach out its nutrients.

Spring: Sheet-compost again, but do it at least a month before planting. Use the compost pile you covered last fall to enrich your early plantings.

Early summer: Between the time of your busiest planting activity and before you move into harvesting, build a large Indore-type compost heap. Plan on leaving this pile undisturbed and covered until the following spring, when it will provide you with plenty of humus.

An alternate plan might involve sheet composting in fall and spring, as described above, and constructing either one or more fast compost piles or an Indore-type heap in midsummer.

The point is: compost, compost, and more compost! You can't take out of your garden what you haven't put in.

COMPOST ENCLOSURES AND BINS

Compost frames are one place where dedicated organic gardeners often let their imaginations and architectural fantasies run wild. Bin and pen designs run the gamut from jerry-rigged knockdown frames made of recycled slats and wire fencing to professionally built concrete block edifices complete with carefully mortared joints, hinged gates and underground catch basins for nutrient-rich runoff water. Humus Taj Mahals!

What kind of compost enclosure does your garden need? Perhaps none at all. Organic matter will rot whether it's housed or not. Didn't the patron saint of compost, Sir Albert Howard, make his classic heaps right on the ground? Good compost depends on assembling the proper variety of materials in the correct proportions, not on frames or bins.

One of the best reasons for enclosing compost in a pen or bin is that the square shape of the contained heap means that more air gets into the pile than in an unenclosed circular pile

Besides, freestanding piles have advantages for some gardeners. Constructing one is certainly a simpler operation, needing nothing more than the organic matter to build the pile, thus saving the cash and time necessary to build an enclosure.

But freestanding piles also have distinct drawbacks. Open heaps take up lots of horizontal space, a considerable loss in a small garden. Unenclosed heaps containing kitchen scraps, unless very carefully constructed and watched over, may also be a magnet for scavengers like dogs and raccoons. And rats.

Also, no matter how carefully built your heaps are, their mere appearance may offend neighbors, especially nongardeners, who might cringe at seeing steaming piles of variegated offal from their dining-room windows.

But if your garden is located on a large lot or if you have nonexistent or understanding neighbors, and if your compostables include little garbage and manure, then an open pile may be a real time- and money-saver.

Most gardeners, however, will choose to house their compost in some type of enclosure. Pens and bins have numerous benefits that offset the expense and effort needed to construct them:

● Bins and pens can be made entirely scavenger-proof

● A well-built enclosure can be an attractive addition to the garden and, depending on the design, can totally disguise its function, thus solving the problem of aesthetics

● Enclosed heaps take up less space. Even a compact garden can house a half ton of compost in a 3 by 3-foot area

● Bins and pens are cubed or rectangular, admitting more air to the decaying materials than a circular heap.

And lastly, a well-built enclosure imposes a kind of discipline on us as gardeners. Because it's a stucture, a compost container is a constant visual reminder to us to tend our humus, to regularly make new batches and to work at improving our soil.

Choosing the Right Kind of Structure

But what kind of bin or pen should you construct? This is no quick decision. Compost receptacles, like any other garden tools, should be adapted to your personal and environmental needs. Most gardeners build a compost structure of some kind, live with it a few seasons and then modify or discard it in favor of a more suitable device. The following discussion should save you from some of this "fine tuning" by helping you see the characteristics of various compost-holding devices.

First, note the difference between bins and pens. Bins are permanent structures of concrete, block or wood

A compost bin is more durable than a pen, but a pen is more portable than a bin

with solid sides and removable fronts. They are stable and scavenger-proof but relatively expensive and time consuming to build. Their siting must be carefully considered, since they cannot be relocated once in place without a hard job of dismantling.

Pens are portable, lightweight structures of wood slats or wood framing and wire fencing or screening. They're easy to dismantle—a blessing when it's time to turn or chop the working compost—and generally admit more air than a solid-sided bin. But their portability also makes them less sturdy and durable.

Compost pits are an alternative to above-ground constructions, though some pits employ a pen or bin to frame the hole. The major benefit of a pit is that it can allow composting to continue well into cold weather; the earth helps shield the contents from freezing temperatures. Pits also provide a ready source of material to cover scraps and organic matter. The huge dirt pile left after excavation can also be covered to stop it from freezing in winter so materials can be added continually. Composting in the ground also means that earthworms have ready access to organic matter.

However, pits are hard to construct. Their use of dirt as a covering also causes them to become anaerobic quickly, although this feature isn't necessarily bad unless you're in a hurry for finished compost. The biggest disadvantage is the difficulty of removing humus. Expect a lot of stooping and shoveling. The finished matter will also be quite heavy because of the large amount of soil mixed in. The pit method is definitely not the right choice for someone with a troublesome back.

Pits are best suited to those gardeners in severe winter areas who wish to extend their composting season and, of course, to those who have the space and inclination to excavate.

Sizes and Sites: What size enclosure will you need? The smallest practical size, as we've seen, is a cubic yard. This basic pile will rot down to about 500 pounds of compost (the actual weight will depend on the materials composted and the pile's moisture content). This quarter ton may sound like a lot of humus, but it's just enough to cover 100 square feet with 3 inches of compost, or three 5 by 20-foot beds an inch deep.

Figure that the minimum amount of compost you'll

need is 1 pound per square foot of garden. So a cubic yard of humus will be adequate for one application on a 500-square-foot growing area. But you can never make too much compost, and one light spreading is hardly enough for a productive season of vegetable growing. You'll also want humus for sidedressing, mulching, potting soil and use on ornamentals. So plan on building either one large heap or succeeding batches throughout the season. You can make a cubic yard of finished compost every three weeks if you've got the organic matter.

A 3 by 3-foot bin full of compost will be enough for one application over a 500-square-foot area

COMPOST FOR CITY DWELLERS: *Town gardeners with small yards can incorporate a simple, unobtrusive compost bin right into the landscape plan. The bin can be tucked into a corner of the yard or along a fence, or hidden behind a shrub or trellised vine.*

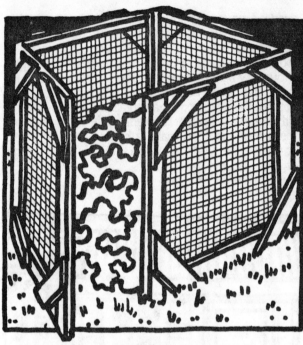

PORTABLE PENS: *A portable pen makes it easy to turn the compost pile. This pen is made of wood and wire fencing, and the four sides simply hook together (above). When you are ready to turn the heap, unlatch the sides of the pen and set it up next to the old pile (top right). Leave the side facing the pile open and simply fork the pile into the pen. Attach the fourth side when the pen is almost full.*

Your bin or pen may be any length or width. Adapt the dimensions to your lot or garden area, but don't build the sides of the enclosure too high. A 4-foot-tall pile is adequate, perhaps ideal, depending on your height and strength. Shoveling or forking materials up onto a heap is hard work, so don't plan on making the pile much over 5 feet tall. Besides, a pile bigger than that can have too much mass. The materials will compress under their own weight, closing the air spaces necessary for effective decomposition.

The shape of your bin or pen may be dictated by the space requirements of your lot or garden. Town gardeners

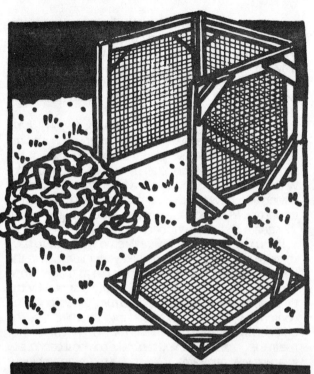

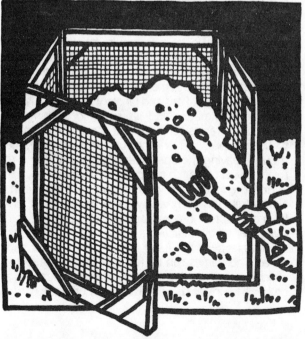

Portable pens can be set up anywhere to make compost right where you need it

often have long narrow yards. There, a rectangular enclosure may make the best use of space. Or a cube-shaped bin, one tucked out of the way of foot traffic, may be best. Of the two, a rectangular shape will expose more of the organic matter to air than a cube, while the latter will present more surface area than a circle.

Be sure to site your enclosure where you'll have enough room to remove organic matter when it's time to turn the heap. Leave plenty of room in front of the receptacle so you're not cramped when trying to work with a pitchfork, shovel and wheelbarrow. Figure on having about two or three times the surface area of the enclosure. (A cubic-yard-size pen would require about 27 square feet of open space in front.)

If you have the room, an ideal setup would be to have three bins side by side. You build your initial pile in the first bin, turning it into the second bin as it ages. Then you begin another heap in the empty first bin. By the time this material is again ready to turn, the second bin's contents will have been tossed into the third bin. The original pile in the third bin will have been removed for use in the garden. Thus, you can make compost continually in a relatively small area. With such a setup, an ambitious gardener could produce several tons of humus every growing season.

You can achieve the same results, however, with only a single portable pen. Let's say you're using wood and wire fencing frame held together by latches (this is the cage pen described in the following section titled How to Make Compost Pens and Bins). After this pen is filled with organic matter and it's ready for turning, you unlatch the frames, remove them and set them up next to the old pile. You only set up three of the frames, though, leaving the open side of the frame facing the heap so you can pitch the material back in.

Add the fourth side of the frame when the pen is almost full. And don't worry about removing the sides from a 4-foot-high compost pile. The heap will stand quite well all by itself, like a giant cake.

Portable pens are ideal for gardeners with ample space. The frames can be hopscotched about, set up exactly where you'll need the finished compost—in an orchard, for instance, or a distant corner of the garden.

Knockdown pens are also a good choice for those who work in community or rental gardens where equipment cannot be left beyond the growing season.

How to Make Compost Pens and Bins

All wood used to make composting structures should be treated with wood preservative. Use a compound known to be nontoxic to plants such as copper naphthenate (sold under the brand name Cuprinol). Creosote is poisonous to plants, especially when it has been freshly applied, but some gardeners report no problems in using creosote-treated lumber in compost bins and frames. In any case, avoid using any preservatives containing pentachlorophenol, which is extremely toxic to plant and animal life, and a compound containing dioxin, one of the most persistent and potent carcinogens. Read the label before you purchase or use any wood preservative.

Here are a number of other points to consider when constructing compost enclosures:

- Bin and pen sides must be strong enough to withstand the powerful lateral pressure of wet organic matter.
- Staple wire or screening to the <u>inside</u> of frames.
- Cleat nail frame parts whenever possible for extra strength. This takes a nail an inch or two longer than the thicknesses of the two pieces of wood to be joined. Drive the nail all the way through the boards, then hammer the protruding part of the nail flat against the wood. It's not pretty, but it's strong. You can also use screws or bolts, but they're more expensive and time consuming.
- All bins and pens should have a lid of some type to protect the compost from rain, which, when excessive, will leach valuable nutrients out of the pile. Covers may be made of old carpeting, weighted-down plastic sheeting, tar paper, scrap metal roofing or wood covers built for the purpose.

It's important to protect compost from rain, which can leach out nutrients; covering the pen or bin solves the problem

Wire Pen: This is the easiest compost enclosure to make. Use a section of wire fencing 11 feet long by 3 to 5 feet high to make a circle 3 feet in diameter. Use three snaps to hold the wire together. (You may also simply

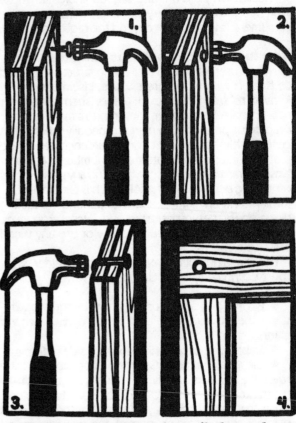

CLEAT-NAILING JOINTS: *Select nails that are longer than the combined thickness of the two boards to be nailed together (top left). Drive the nail completely through the two boards (top right). Hammer the protruding nail end flat against the board (bottom left). This method for joining boards provides maximum strength for the joined parts.*

twist the wire ends together when you form the loop, but twisting them apart when the bin is full will be hard on your fingers.)

Choose narrow mesh fencing with openings measuring 1 by 2 inches or smaller. A wider mesh will let much of your compost fall through the sides. If you must use a larger mesh like concrete reinforcing wire (which has 6

WIRE PEN: *A simple cylinder of hardware cloth or fencing wire is the easiest kind of compost enclosure to make. Fasten the ends of the pen together with snaps, clips, or wire, or just tie them with rope or twine.*

by 6-inch openings), you can line the inside of the pen with roll roofing. Wire it to the inside of the fencing, and pierce it with numerous ventilation holes.

Snow Fencing Pen: Snow fencing is usually made of 2-inch-wide wood slats that are 4 feet high. The slats are wired together to form a flexible fencing. A 10-foot section can be easily formed into a freestanding circle, though you may need a few steel fence posts driven in around the perimeter to hold the fencing in place until it's filled with organic matter.

Snow fencing has one drawback as a compost enclosure. It's made to slow the advance of blowing snow, not wet organic matter. The lightweight wood slats will rot rapidly as the acids in humus begin to digest them. So don't rush out to buy a roll of snow fencing specifically to make a compost pen. Use scraps of discarded fencing (check with your highway department); otherwise, depend on materials with a longer service life.

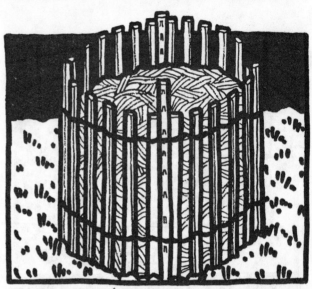

SNOW FENCE PEN: *Arrange a 10-foot section of snow fencing into a free-standing circle. Drive four steel fence posts around the perimeter to hold the fence in place when the compost is added.*

Wood Pallet Pen: Over a million wood pallets are thrown away every year in this country, a shocking waste of wood. You can easily reclaim many of these sturdy platforms from dumps and from businesses that might otherwise discard them. A drive through an industrial section of any town should turn up at least four pallets, which is all that you need to make a free, long-lasting pen.

Tie or wire three pallets together to make an open pen. You may also secure them with heavy-duty hooks and eyes or lengths of chain and snaps.

Shovel or fork your compostables into the pen until it's about half full. Then attach the front pallet and continue filling the bin. When it's time to turn or remove the contents, simply dismantle the pen and set it up in its new location.

Note that pallets come in various sizes and weights. Some, built for big loads, are made of heavy timbers and may take two people to wrestle into position. Shop around for relatively lightweight pallets. For longer life,

To make a pen from wood pallets, look for pallets that are relatively light in weight

WOOD PALLET PEN: *Tie three pallets together to make an open pen. Fill the pen half full with your compostables; then attach the fourth pallet and finish filling the pen. This pen can be easily disassembled and set up in a new location when it is time to turn.*

treat the wood with preservative that is nontoxic to plants.

Cage Pens: These screened bins are good looking, durable, scavenger-proof and portable. They also allow excellent air circulation.

Use 2 by 2's, 2 by 4's or lumber of a similar size to build four frames of whatever size you prefer. A frame 4 feet high by 6 feet wide will yield about 18 cubic feet of compost every three weeks if you make hot compost as described previously.

Use care in building the frame sides so they'll last for many seasons. Lap the joints if you can, using a router, table saw or chisel and mallet. Attach gussets to all four corners (use scraps of plywood or 1 by 2's) for additional strength.

Attach wire screening to the <u>inside</u> of each frame (with gussets on the outside) using heavy-duty staples. For extra strength you might also nail slats over the

STRENGTHENING CAGE PENS: *For cage pens, attach gussets to all four corners to strengthen joints and increase durability.*

stapled area. For screening use ½-inch chicken wire or hardware cloth. Screening with larger openings is cheaper but less able to withstand the outward pressure of wet compost.

When all the frame sides are constructed, latch three together with screen-door hooks and eyes. Leave the front of the frame unhooked until the bin is half full. Then latch on the fourth side.

The New Zealand Bin: This popular design is so named because it was first built by members of the Auckland Humic Club. The structure is simple and attractive and allows plenty of air circulation. It is, however, made entirely of lumber, which may make it expensive unless you use scraps or rough cut boards purchased at a sawmill.

The basic design is 4 feet square and 4 feet high or slightly higher. The corner posts are not sunk into the ground, but the New Zealand bin should be considered a permanent structure since the sides don't come apart.

You'll need four 2 by 4's, each 4 feet long. Lay two 2 by 4's on the ground or your work table, and nail 1 by 6

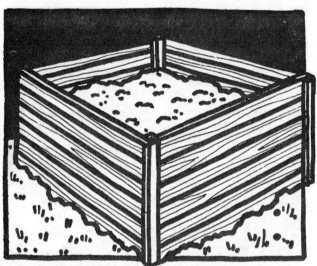

NEW ZEALAND BIN: *This bin, made entirely from lumber, measures 4 feet square and 4 feet high. The half-inch air space between the boards allows for maximum air circulation.*

slats across, forming one side of the bin. Leave a half-inch space between each slat for ventilation.

Build another side the same way. Then add another 2 by 4 to each side, forming a channel for the front boards, which slide up and down.

When both sides are complete, stand them on end, and nail on the boards forming the back of the bin, again leaving air spaces between the slats.

Slide in the front boards as the pile grows. To get air circulation between the front slats, you'll need to glue or nail spacer blocks on the top edge of each board. A piece of scrap 1 by 2 lumber about 3 inches long fastened to the ends of each board works fine.

The New Zealand bin can also be built using 6-foot-long 2 by 4's, sinking them 1 foot into the ground for greater stability.

It's important to note that any freestanding pen or open front bin except those made of concrete, block or heavy timbers will tend to bow outward as the compost absorbs moisture and settles. This expansion may pop the nails out of the slats and, at the least, will make it

To allow for air circulation in the New Zealand bin, which has solid sides, make the front of the bin out of sliding boards with space between them

FRONT OF NEW ZEALAND BIN: *Although basically a permanent structure, the front of the New Zealand bin is designed so that the boards slide in and out along a channel. As the pile grows, more boards can be added.*

hard to slide the front boards in and out of the channels.

You can make a simple device to combat bowing. You'll need a 4-foot-long piece of 2 by 4 (if your bin is 4 feet square). Nail a 2 by 4 by 2-inch block of wood at each end of this piece. Then lay it across the top of the bin (with the end blocks hugging the top slats) as you fill the bin. This antibowing device can also be moved forward to accommodate a bin cover.

The Lehigh Bin: This attractive, easily built bin is another classic compost-making structure. Like the New Zealand bin, it also is made of 2 by 4's. To house a cubic yard of compost you'll need 20 36-inch-long 2 by 4's (five per side).

Measure 2 inches in from the end of each board and drill a ⅜-inch-diameter hole. The boards are alternated and held together by steel rods slipped through the holes. To ensure exact alignment of these holes, it's best to make a cardboard template. Also, use a drill press or drill jig to assure a straight hole.

ANTI-BOWING DEVICE: *This simple device keeps free-standing pens, or bins made of weak material, from bowing. For a bin 4 feet square, nail a 2 by 4-inch block of wood to each end of a 4-foot-long 2 by 4. Lay it across the top of the bin with the end blocks pressing against the top slats.*

Don't buy expensive finished lumber for this bin. Use rough cut wood or 3-inch-diameter poles. If you have wooded area on your property, thinning a large stand of saplings may yield all the wood you'll need for this project.

The Lehigh bin is easy to use because you can build the sides up as you increase the height of the pile. This same feature is a disadvantage, however, if you expect to turn the pile regularly. Because the slats alternate, the bin must be totally disassembled before you can remove the compost.

The Lehigh bin is a good choice, therefore, for compost piles needing little or no turning.

Modular Slat Bin or Pen: This enclosure combines features of both bin and pen, having the sturdiness of a bin and the knockdown portability of a pen. This is also a stackable structure that will grow in height as your compost pile increases in size.

The modular slat bin is stackable and comes apart easily so it can be stored flat over the winter

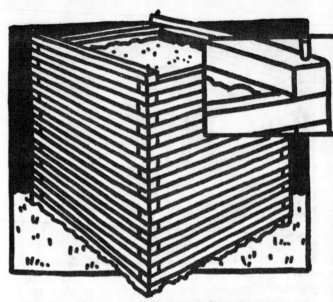

LEHIGH BIN: *To assemble the bin, drill holes in the ends of the 2 by 4's, alternate the boards and slip a steel rod through the holes to hold the boards together.*

At season's end all the sections may be quickly dismantled and stored flat for the winter. (This is another good choice for those who garden in rental or community plots where all equipment must be removed in fall.)

Each modular section consists of four boards 50½ inches long and approximately 10 inches wide. The following directions and materials will help you build enough modules to construct a bin 37 inches tall by 50½ inches square.

You'll need 8 pieces of 10-foot-long 1 by 10's. Cut each of these in half to get 16 boards 5 feet long. Measure 4 inches in from the end of each board and mark a line 4⅝ inches across the board's width. Cut a slot at that point, making it wide enough so you can easily slide another board into it. Repeat the procedure with the other end of the board. Each board should have two slots.

When all the slots are cut, fit the boards together like puzzle parts—no nails, screws or glue are needed. Stack the modules as you heap up the compost.

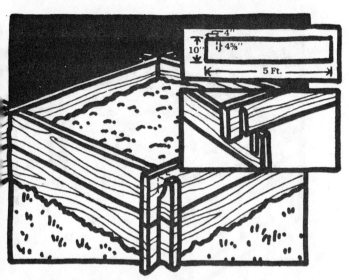

MODULAR SLAT BIN: *This movable bin is constructed solely with wood planks; it is easy to assemble, disassemble and store. The ends of the boards are slotted to fit together at right angles.*

Three-Compartment Block Bin. This is the Rolls Royce of compost enclosures. It's time consuming to build but is well worth the effort.

To build a three-compartment bin 4 feet wide by 12 feet long by 3 feet high, you'll need 88 concrete blocks and 20 half blocks. (Full blocks measure 6 by 8 by 16 inches.)

The first course of block must be laid level to ensure that succeeding courses are plumb; this is especially important because you won't be using mortar to hold the blocks in place. Also, be sure to use the half blocks to stagger all joints.

Measure off the 12-foot back wall lines and the four 4-foot-wide side walls. Use stakes and string to mark these lines. Then scrape away all the grass and brush where the blocks will lay. Dig out any roots or rocks. Then begin laying blocks for the 12-foot back wall. Work carefully, fitting each block into place, digging away underneath if necessary to get a level course. Use a mason's level—one that spans at least two concrete blocks—to check your work. (Better yet is a 4-foot level,

When building a block bin, use a mason's level to make sure the blocks are laid on a level course

TONS OF HUMUS WITH A THREE-COMPARTMENT BLOCK BIN: *These permanent, sturdy bins provide the ideal setup to make several tons of humus every growing season. You can start compost in the bins at staggered times to provide a continuing supply of humus through the growing season.*

available for a nominal fee at most rental tool shops.)

When the first course of block for the back wall is in place, lay out the two outside side walls. Be sure the corners form a 90-degree angle. Check this with a framing square. Then lay out the blocks for the two inside walls, checking the plumb and square as you work.

With the last course completed and level, lay up the rest of the blocks, using the half blocks where appropriate. Once all the blocks are in place, you may want to enclose the front of the bin with movable boards. There are several ways to do this.

The easiest technique is to use a sheet of scrap plywood, particle board or fencing. Nail a 4-inch-long piece of 1 by 2 in the center as a cleat. When you want to close off the bin, lay the sheet against the opening with the cleat on the outside. Force a stick or pipe

SIMPLE FRONT FOR BLOCK BIN: *Take a 4-inch-long piece of 1 by 2, and nail it in the center of a sheet of scrap plywood large enough to cover the front of the bin. To close off the bin, lay the board against the opening of the bin with the cleat on the outside. Prop a stick or pipe up against the cleat to hold the board in place.*

under this cleat to hold the sheet in place.

For more aesthetically pleasing bin gates you can install removable boards. This arrangement will let you vary the height of the front gates as the pile grows.

Attach 1 by 6 boards to the front of each column of blocks, securing the lumber with long toggle bolts. (Use a carbide-tipped bit to drill through the blocks into the hollow sections.)

Next, nail a 2 by 4 vertically to each 1 by 6. Use nails and glue for extra strength. Center the 2 by 4's carefully so you have equal space on each side. Then nail another 1 by 6 to the 2 by 4, again centering carefully.

This design gives you a 2-inch-wide channel, enough to accommodate several sliding 1 by 12's or 1 by 10's. The groove is intentionally made an inch wider than the sliding boards to compensate for the pressure exerted by the compost as each bin fills. (You'll need the extra

CHANNEL FOR FRONT GATE OF BLOCK BIN: *Attach 1 by 6 boards to the front of each column of block with long toggle bolts. Center a 2 by 4 vertically on each of the 1 by 6's so there is equal space on each side. Nail another 1 by 6 to the 2 by 4, centering carefully. The front boards slide easily between the 1 by 6's, allowing you to increase the height of the front gate as the pile grows.*

space to wiggle the boards as you remove them.)

Glue a 3-inch piece of scrap 1 by 2 to each end of the sliding boards as spacers to increase air circulation through the front of the bin.

Wood Bin: Here's a bin with the same design as the one above, but it's made entirely of wood, which may be less expensive for some gardeners than concrete block.

Measure off the perimeter of the bin—12 feet long and 4 feet wide—by marking the corners with string and stakes or by simply marking lines on the ground with the edge of a spade. Sink eight treated 4 by 4 by 6-foot-long posts at least 2 feet into the ground at each corner. You can set the posts directly into the ground, tamping the dirt around them, or you can cement them in place for the longest life and usefulness.

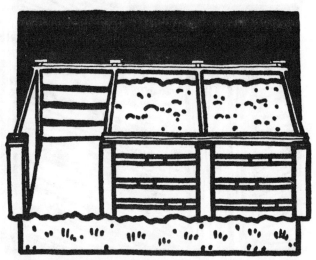

WOOD BIN: *Identical in design to the block bin, this bin can be less expensive to construct when made with wood. Leave 1- to 2-inch spaces between the boards to allow for ventilation. The front can be made of sliding boards, as for the block bin, but you can eliminate the 1 by 6 spacers, nailing the 2 by 4's directly to the end posts to form the channels.*

Use a level to get the posts plumb before making their position permanent. Next, nail the horizontal boards in place all around the bin (except in front), leaving a space of an inch or two between each board for ventilation.

Make front gates as with the block bin, only here you can skip the face plates (the 1 by 6 boards) by nailing or screwing the 2 by 4's directly to the posts, then nailing the covering 1 by 6 boards over these.

The Compost Pit: This is a lot of work at the outset, but once completed you'll have an all-weather, permanent, large-capacity composting site. The compost pit is a good choice for large homesteads, farms or inns producing a lot of kitchen scraps.

Dig a pit 4 by 4 feet square and 16 inches deep. Make the pit sides flat enough to line with cinder blocks. Lay three unmortared courses of three blocks on each side. Two courses of block will be below ground level; one

If you have a lot of kitchen scraps or other material to compost, a pit may be the best solution

FRONT GATE FOR WOOD BIN: *To make a gate for a wood bin, nail 2 by 4's directly to the end posts, centering as you would for the block bin. Finish with 1 by 6 boards nailed to the 2 by 4's. The front gate boards can be slid in and out of the channel.*

will be above. (Build the pit close to your house so you won't have to haul garbage long distances in winter.)

Carefully mound up all the excavated dirt. Cover it with a tarp, plastic sheeting or old hay or straw to protect it from rain. Throw each load of garbage into the pit, then level and cover it with 3 inches of soil from the pile. Add earthworms whenever possible (the kind found in your garden). They will multiply rapidly and feed on the scraps.

Cover the garbage-dirt accumulation with burlap bags or other porous material, not lumber or metal. Keep the burlap moistened by sprinkling it with water when necessary. As in the traditional compost pile, the object is to keep the decomposing materials moist but not saturated.

To make the pit scavenger-proof, make a frame of 1 by 2's or 1 by 3's, covering it with a 2 by 3-inch mesh heavy gauge fencing, the kind called "turkey wire." Make the frame large enough to sit flat on the blocks. Weight it down with rocks or a cinder block.

CINDER BLOCK PIT: *Using a cinder-block-lined pit allows you to compost through the winter months. Line a 4 by 4-foot-square pit that is 16 inches deep with cinder blocks; two layers below ground level, one above. Mound up all excavated soil next to the pit and cover with a protective material to prevent freezing.*

This compost pit can expand as you accumulate more organic matter. Just add another course of blocks every time the garbage and dirt mixture becomes level with the first course of blocks. You can keep adding courses until you reach a height of 32 inches. After that the pit gets too hard to fill. Of course, you can stop filling the pit whenever you wish. You don't need to turn the material; just let the contents decompose for about three months in mild weather before using them in your garden.

If this structure meets your needs, you'll want to start a second pit or bin while you wait for the first to finish working. With experience, you'll learn to top off the second pit just as the contents of your first pit are ready to add to the garden.

Freezing weather will slow decomposition, but you can keep on adding garbage all winter. Just make sure your dirt pile doesn't freeze solid. Cover it with plenty of old hay or straw bales or bags of dead leaves. A deep snow cover will also add insulation.

SCREEN COVER FOR PIT: *Scavenger-proof your pit by constructing a wire-covered frame that sits on top of the blocks. Rocks are placed on all four corners to weight it down.*

You can continue to compost during the winter as long as the pile doesn't freeze solid; covering it with hay or bags of dry leaves will help insulate the heap

There's no need to cover the pit with burlap bags in winter. Moisture retention isn't a problem in cold weather. Nor must you remove the snow that builds up on the pile. But do keep the wire frame in place at all times to stop marauding animals from digging in the pit.

Unusual Enclosures and Containers

In addition to the basic designs described, gardeners have traditionally used all kinds of arrangements to hold compost. Here are three further suggestions. Their virtues are simplicity and low cost. Their drawbacks are their appearance, lack of capacity or inconvenience.

Hay Bales: You can use bales of hay like giant blocks to create a large bin or an enclosure of whatever size you prefer. If you're adventurous and the bales are tightly bound, you can stack them two or three high.

Don't expect this makeshift container to last very long, though. The bales and the binder twine will be composting right along with the rest of the heap. When the bales collapse and fall apart, you can use them to start the next heap.

Steel Drums: Steel drums are readily available from a

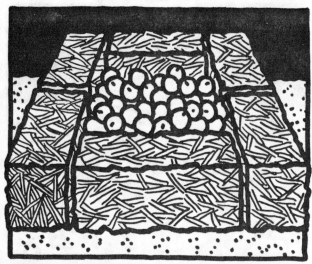

HAY BALE ENCLOSURE: *Hay bales can be used to make a very inexpensive but temporary enclosure. Arrange the hay bales to make an enclosure however large you desire. This is not a durable structure, as the binder twine and hay itself will decompose as well as the contents.*

variety of sources, but it is very important to obtain barrels that haven't held toxic materials. Check with car washes (for drums that previously held biodegradable soap) or food processing plants (for drums that have held vegetable oil or molasses). Cut out the top of the drum with a saber saw that is fitted with a metal-cutting blade. Wear goggles and ear protectors.

Drill numerous holes on the sides and bottom of the drum for aeration. Fashion a cover out of scrap lumber. Set it on top of the drum and weight it down with a cinder block.

Fill the drum with organic matter, layering wet and dry materials or mixing them thoroughly to even out the moisture content. Kitchen scraps in particular should be mixed with sawdust or shredded dead leaves to offset their extreme wetness. Kitchen scraps that are simply dumped into the barrel and left uncovered will produce incredibly bad odors as the whole mess goes anaerobic.

No turning is done with the contents of the drum

STEEL DRUMS FOR COMPOSTING: *Drill holes in the sides and bottom of a steel drum. Fill with compostables and cover with a piece of scrap lumber weighted down with a rock or cinder block. When ready to use, tip the barrel onto its side and shovel out the contents.*

unless you want to use it as a holding bin for collecting organic matter until you have enough on hand to make a full-size pile. The drum can only be emptied by pushing it over on its side and shoveling it out. Some gardeners have several of these drums on hand, filling them and letting them sit for months until decomposition is complete.

Compost can be made in plastic trash bags by an anaerobic process, but you must take care not to open the bags before the compost is finished

Plastic Bags: Although they are particularly ugly when left out in view, plastic bags are remarkably effective. A sealed plastic bag filled with damp organic matter is like an artificial stomach. Filled with green grass clippings and placed in a warm spot, the bags will produce what looks and smells like genuine manure.

The breakdown process is anaerobic and quite slow. And, of course, no turning of materials is necessary. Fill the bags with grass clippings and dead leaves (and manure, if you have it) and set them out of the way with their tops gathered up tightly and sealed. Don't fill them with kitchen scraps unless you're sure your yard is entirely protected against scavenging dogs and raccoons. Otherwise, these creatures will tear the bags apart and scatter the contents.

Forget about the bags for at least several months. When you do open the sacks you should have thoroughly digested "manure" ready for the garden. Let your nose and eyes be the guide. If you open the bags too soon you'll be greeted with a horrid stink and more slime than you've seen since your last horror movie.

Obviously, composting-in-a-bag has several liabilities aside from the aesthetics of living with lots of bloated black plastic "stomachs" littering your landscape. One is volume: the bags don't hold much. Another is fragility: the thin plastic won't last long if exposed to the elements. But if you only need a small amount of compost and prefer not to build a traditional heap, plastic bags may work well in your garden.

A Reservoir for Compost Water

Of all the elixirs, mixtures, potions and notions organic gardeners have dreamed up to nourish their plants, nothing beats the effectiveness of compost or manure teas. Such homemade liquid plant food has an almost magical power to increase flagging vegetable production, to rejuvenate sickly plants and trees and to stimulate growth of tender seedlings and transplants.

Many of the plant nutrients found in compost and manure dissolve easily in water, so thirsty roots can quickly take them up. Compost water is easy to make on a small scale. You need only dump a shovelful of manure or finished compost into a bucket of water, swish it around and pour the liquid at the base of your plants.

That's fine for a tiny garden or a house plant collection, but what do you do when you want to feed your crops compost tea on a regular basis, perhaps every week throughout the growing season? You can give heavy feeders like eggplant, tomatoes and cabbage a needed boost with compost tea, especially in midseason, when their production is slowing down. But you're going to need a reservoir of compost water to do this. Stopping to make a bucketful whenever you need one is just another time-consuming task in an already busy season.

Using compost water is a convenient way to give heavy-feeding crops a midseason fertilizer boost

Nor do you want exposed tubs or half barrels brimming with manure water sitting around the garden. Distracted children and gardeners have a knack for falling into such traps.

You can easily make a compost or manure water barrel that will last for years and keep your plants awash in good nutrition. The following design will instantly give you gallons of liquid plant food with the twist of a faucet. Plus no splashing, dripping or splatter.

You'll need a 55-gallon steel drum free of any harmful residues. Check your local car wash for discarded drums that have held biodegradable soap. Feed stores are another possible source. They often have drums that have held stock food. Look also for drums that have held cooking oil, syrup or other nontoxic substances.

Cut out the top of the barrel using a saber saw fitted with a metal-cutting blade. Wear ear and eye protectors for this job. Discard the cut-out top and thoroughly wash out the drum.

Turn the barrel on its side and stabilize it with logs or cinder blocks. What comes next will make a boiler factory sound like chamber music; make sure you warn your neighbors, and put on your ear protectors. Using a ball peen hammer, flatten an area of the drum's side about 2 or 3 inches up from the bottom. The actual area of this flattened space isn't critical, but be sure you level a spot at least 4 inches in diameter. Go slowly on this task. You want a flat place to ensure that the faucet you'll install makes a flush, leak-proof fit. If you misjudge and whack the drum side too hard, you can crawl into the barrel and hammer out the bulge again.

Once you have a reasonably flat spot hammered out, sandpaper the area to a bright finish, removing all paint and rust. Now take a steel nipple—6 inches long, ¾ inch in diameter, threaded on both ends—and stand it upright on the flattened area about 2 inches up from the drum's bottom. Use a pencil or scribe to carefully trace around the nipple's end, marking the outline on the drum. Drill a pilot hole through the center of this circle large enough to admit the metal-cutting saber saw blade.

Now comes some tricky cutting. The object is to cut a hole slightly smaller than the threaded end of the nipple so the pipe can be screwed snugly into the hole.

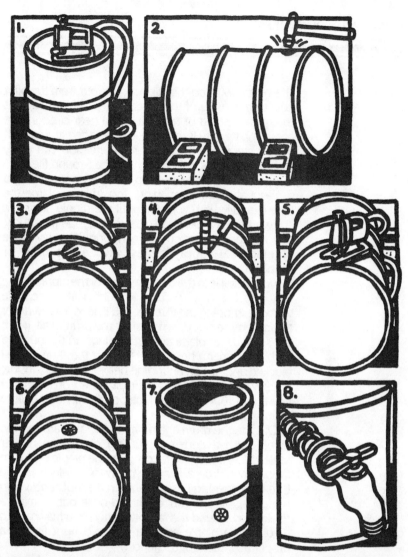

INSTALLING A FAUCET IN A DRUM: *There are seven easy steps in installing a faucet in a steel drum to make a reservoir for compost water. 1. Cut out the top of the steel drum with a saber saw. 2. Turn the barrel on its side and support with cinder blocks on each side. Flatten out a circular area 4 inches in diameter, 2 to 3 inches from the bottom, with a ball peen hammer. 3. Sandpaper the flattened area until it has a bright finish. 4. Stand the nipple upright on the flat area and trace around its end. 5. Drill a pilot hole through the center of the circle large enough to admit the metal-cutting saber saw. 6. Cut a hole slightly smaller than the end of the nipple. Do this by cutting slits out from the hole to the inside of the scribed line. File the rough edges to get a snug fit. 7. Assemble the nipple and faucet parts, shown in the detail (8).*

The best way to do this is to cut slits out from the pilot hole to the <u>inside</u> of the scribed line, nibbling away at the metal instead of trying to cut a neat circle in one pass. Don't worry if the hole looks ragged at first with bits of metal "teeth" here and there. You can easily clean these away with a round or half-round file.

Try screwing the nipple into the hole once you've got a reasonably round opening. Too small? Enlarge the hole carefully with your file until the nipple begins to screw in tightly. Once you're sure the pipe fits snugly, remove it and thread on a ¾-inch conduit nut (available at electrical supply stores) and a flat fiber or rubber washer.

Now crawl into the drum and screw the nipple all the way into the hole, getting as tight a fit as possible without stripping the threads. You'll need a screwdriver to tighten the nut down against the drum wall. (Push the screwdriver blade against the lugs on the nut. Tap with a hammer if necessary.) Be sure the drum is well blocked and not on an incline <u>before</u> you crawl inside; otherwise you may find yourself on an unscheduled ride down your driveway. (The police will never believe your excuse.)

Outside the drum again, smear the area around the nipple with a generous coating of silicone rubber sealer. Now screw the faucet onto the nipple end. (The faucet should be a flange type with a ¾-inch female threaded opening.) As you tighten the faucet down on the drum, silicone rubber should ooze out, forming a thick bead around the faucet's flange. You may have to readjust the nipple and nut to get a tight fit and a proper alignment of the faucet.

After you've installed the faucet, don't forget to cover the pipe opening inside the drum with a piece of fiberglass screening; this will keep the pipe from clogging

Don't worry if the hole in the drum is too large or eccentric. A liberal dose of silicone should seal any leaks. For an extra strong fitting you can seal the faucet in place with a glob of liquid steel. When that's dry, follow with a doping of silicone sealer.

Once the faucet is in place, crawl back into the drum with a stainless steel pipe clamp, a screwdriver and a 6-inch-square piece of fiberglass screening. Wrap the screening around the pipe opening, and tighten the clamp in place. This will stop any solids from clogging the faucet.

Let the silicone or liquid steel dry for at least 24 hours.

In the meantime, build a platform or base for the barrel out of scrap lumber. I used 2 by 4's for the legs and sides and ¾-inch exterior plywood for the top. The dimensions aren't critical. Just be sure that the top is wide enough to fully support the filled drum, that the legs are slightly splayed to distribute the weight, and that the platform raises the drum high enough to fit a watering can or bucket under the faucet.

If the ground where your drum will sit gets spongy during wet weather, you may want to put bricks or patio blocks under the platform legs to ensure a strong foundation. A fully loaded manure water barrel will weigh over 400 pounds, and you'll want it firmly in place.

When your platform is completed and the silicone sealer is dry, you may wish to paint the drum with a rust-resistant paint. Do, at least, paint over the area you sanded down to bare metal. Then choose a site for the drum that is either in the garden itself or as close as possible to it in order to minimize lugging pails of manure water and fertilizing your socks all summer.

Set the platform and barrel up the way you want it, then prepare a giant tea bag. Fill an old feed sack with fresh manure, aged compost or both. Add whatever organic materials you have on hand. Don't worry much about proportions. I make a wild "kickapoo joy juice" using goat and horse manure, compost, nettles, comfrey and a few handfuls of rock phosphate, granite dust, blood meal and granular seaweed.

Tie off the top of the sack and lower it into the drum. Fill the barrel with water and let the mixture steep for at least several days, the longer the better. Be sure to cover the drum with a sheet of plastic, securing it with an elastic shock cord. Or create your own drum cover of wood or metal. But do use a tight-fitting cover of some kind, or your barrel will become a breeding pond for clouds of mosquitoes.

There's no secret to using manure or compost water. Some gardeners like to dilute the mixture, adding water to create a tea-colored liquid. Others use compost water full-strength (the solution won't burn plant roots). Of course, diluting the mixture makes it go farther, which means you won't have to refill the barrel as often.

The drum can usually be filled with water twice using

After making compost water, don't throw the compost away; use it as a mulch, or dig it into the garden

the same sack of organic materials. After that the mixture becomes too diluted to do much good. But nothing goes to waste in an organic garden, so don't discard that spent compost. It's still a valuable soil conditioner. Dig it in, or use it as mulch.

And here's a tip for the adventurous gardener who has some elevated ground adjoining his or her garden. Perhaps there's a hill or retaining wall nearby. Setting the manure water drum above the garden would put gravity to work, not requiring you to apply compost tea by the ladleful. You could screw a hose onto the faucet and actually water your plants with nourishing compost tea!

Where to Store Compost Materials until You're Ready to Build the Heap

What do you do with your kitchen scraps until you have enough accumulated to make compost? If you're making compost every four weeks, you'll need a fly- and odor-free means of storing your raw materials until you can consign them to a heap. Which method you use to accomplish this depends on where and how you live.

If yours is a rural setting with plenty of room, you can build a predator-proof holding bin designed for the safe storage of scraps. The sides of this bin must be made of concrete, block or rot-resistant lumber. You'll also need a lid of heavy screening or fencing. Cover each day's dumping of wastes with sawdust, shavings, soil or leaves to discourage flies.

All you're really doing here is building a compost pile by degrees. It won't heat up until you've assembled enough materials—a minimum of a cubic yard—so be sure to mix and layer the ingredients as you add them. When you've accumulated sufficient kitchen scraps, add more absorbent matter and begin creating a full-size compost pile.

The city or suburban gardener has more potential problems when storing kitchen scraps. Flies, rats, stray dogs and irate neighbors all become quickly aware of improperly deposited garbage. But you can avoid all these hassles if you'll follow the advice of Bill and Helga Olkowski, authors of The City People's Book of Raising Food:

1. Get some 5-gallon cans. Used drywall compound cans are perfect for this. They're plastic, come with

snap-on lids, and are discarded by the truckload. Check at your local dump and at construction sites, or ask a drywall contractor.

2. Obtain some fine-grained sawdust. Cabinetmakers and carpenters may give you all you'll need for free. Sawmills can supply you with a rough grade sawdust that will also do. If sawdust is unavailable, use soil, sand, wood ashes or dry leaves.

3. Dump each day's scraps into a 5-gallon can. Immediately cover the wastes with no less than an inch of sawdust. Cover the can tightly. Be sure you can detect no odor. (Flies zero in on garbage odors. No stink means no flies.)

4. When the can is almost full, cover the last layer of scraps with more sawdust and snap the lid on. Set the can aside until you accumulate enough to build a full-size pile.

The full cans may be stored in any convenient place until you're ready to build the pile. Drywall compound cans in particular are completely animal-proof. Hose out the cans after emptying them.

STORING KITCHEN SCRAPS: *Kitchen debris of apartment or city gardeners can be stored in 5-gallon cans. Dump daily kitchen refuse in the can and cover with a 1-inch layer of fine-grained sawdust. Place the lid on tightly. When the can is nearly full, put an extra-thick layer of sawdust on top, replace the lid and put aside until you have enough to build a full-size compost pile.*

HOW AND WHEN TO USE COMPOST

There's no mystery to using compost. You can't put on too much or apply it too frequently. It won't burn or otherwise harm your plants or soil. And it's certainly not harmful to the environment! Indeed, the main problem most gardeners have with compost is that they can't get enough of it.

Use only finished compost around growing plants; unfinished compost is best used in parts of the garden that have already been harvested

When to Apply Compost

First, check the condition of the pile. Is the material only partially decomposed? Half-finished compost, like all raw or partially decomposed organic matter, will tie up some of the soil nitrogen until it decays completely. So use partially rotted materials in garden areas where you've already harvested and don't plan to reseed, as will be the case in late summer or early fall.

This time of the year is also best for soil-building practices in general. Turn under plenty of compost, finished or not, plus dead leaves, plant wastes (if undiseased), manure, grass clippings and fruit wastes left from canning and freezing. This is sheet composting, of course, and winter's freezing and thawing will mellow whatever you dig in by spring, leaving the soil rich in nutrients for your early plantings.

During the garden season proper, it's best to add rough or still fibrous compost about a month before actually planting. This gives the material time to break down further. But you can work fine textured compost into your soil closer to planting time, even using it on the day you transplant or seed. This advice applies to adding compost directly to your soil, not using it as a mulch.

Any mulching material tends to keep the soil cool, so spreading a layer of compost around early plantings of tomatoes, for example, would slow growth rather than stimulating it. Use compost as a mulch for heat-loving plants only after the soil has fully warmed up in late spring or early summer.

But some plants like "cool feet" — peas, members of the cabbage family and potatoes, for example. An early spring layer of compost would benefit them, particularly if your summers come early and stay hot.

In general, fall, early winter and early spring are the optimum times to incorporate large amounts of compost, not so much for the garden's sake as for yours, the gardener's. These months are the least crowded with chores, so you can concentrate more fully on soil building without being pulled away to do seeding or harvesting. You'll also have less chance of damaging your established plants by digging materials in around them.

If your soil is particularly poor in structure or fertility, lay the organic matter on heavily in the fall. Work as much as you can into the top 12 to 18 inches, using compost or fresh materials like manure, dead leaves, hay or vegetable and fruit scraps. Leave the soil surface rough. The fibrous matter will help anchor the soil against wind and water erosion. Putting this organic matter deeper in the soil helps distribute humus throughout the root zone, assuring the presence of moisture and nutrients in solution.

If your soil is poor, dig in lots of compost in fall, and you will see improvement when you're ready to plant in spring

Don't curse your poor soil. Pick up your spade instead. A 3-inch layer of compost dug in 6 inches deep every year will transform depleted soil in only three garden seasons.

Spreading compost just before you till, plow or dig your garden in the spring is another wise procedure. Mixing the organic matter with the slowly warming earth supplies food to those rapidly multiplying soil organisms. This community of microbes, so vital to plant health, becomes lively and reproduces when the soil temperature rises to about 32°F. But when the ground warms to 50°F and above, the organisms shift into the intense activity typical of a healthy soil. So applying compost in the early spring means the organic matter will be available to feed bacteria, fungi and other life forms just as they begin to increase their activity and multiplication.

That's also a good reason for laying on the compost and natural rock powders in summer, when the soil's microbial population approaches its most dynamic state. Plants demand more nourishment from the soil in warm weather, but this is also the time when the soil has the most to give, precisely because soil bacteria and other organisms are furiously active, breaking down organic and mineral matter, making the nutrients available to plants.

So it makes sense to spread compost and rock dust in summer, feeding it directly to soil organisms and plants hungry for fresh material. Organic fertilizers and soil conditioners of all kinds (humus, granite dust, phosphate rock, greensand, bone meal) are also needed most in summer because they help the soil retain moisture and oxygen. Of course, adding these materials at any time of the year is a wise garden investment. Your plants will thrive during the growing season and your soil will increase its long-term reserve of nutrients.

How to Apply Compost
In applying compost, a general rule of thumb (a green thumb, of course) is to spread ½ inch to 3 inches over growing areas once or twice during the growing season. Unless you're using compost as mulch, mix it into the top 4 inches of earth, where soil organisms are most active. You can do this by hand, with a shovel or spading fork, or with a rotary tiller.

When topdressing vegetable plants, work the compost into the soil no deeper than an inch to avoid injuring delicate roots

Using Compost in the Vegetable Garden:
Vegetables thrive when they're grown in compost-rich soil. Some people say they taste better, too. One reason this may be so is indicated in recent research, which shows that plants grown in humusy soil tend to absorb minerals more efficiently than plants grown with synthetic fertilizers.

There are several specific ways to use compost in your

vegetable garden. You can work it into the soil as already suggested, incorporating liberal amounts in the early spring about a month before planting. But also use finished compost as a sidedressing throughout the growing season. Apply it in bands between rows or as rings around plants. Work it lightly into the soil, being careful not to dig too deeply around the base of your plants. Work the humus only into the top inch or so of the soil to avoid injuring feeder roots near the surface.

Applying compost as a sidedressing before a rain is another good idea, as is watering in the humus with a hose. Deeply soaking compost washes many soluble nutrients down into the root zone, supplying plants with some easily absorbed food.

SIDE-DRESSING WITH COMPOST: *Apply finished compost in bands between rows or as rings around individual plants. Work it into the soil about 1 inch deep. Do this very carefully, trying not to disturb the delicate root systems.*

You can also use compost liberally just before you set out transplants or plant seeds. The following is a method that I've used for a number of years with outstanding results. When planting peas, beans, corn and cucumbers, I begin by digging a furrow 4 inches deep, and filling it with 2 inches of finished compost. The next step is to rake in about an inch of topsoil, then I plant and cover my seeds. Finally I water the area heavily (at least a gallon per square foot) unless I expect a significant amount of rain within 24 hours.

USING COMPOST WATER

You might want to store some compost water in plastic jugs over the winter (or make it in your basement) for use in early spring when you're starting plants for the garden. Greenhouse operators and commercial growers use compost tea as a starter solution for seedlings. Liquid compost gives plants an immediate shot of nourishment—an important booster, especially after transplanting.

Try soaking seeds in compost water. Some research demonstrates that seeds treated this way show improved germination. And why not? Aren't seeds in a natural setting soaked in humus water? You can even soak the entire flat by placing it in a larger container holding compost water. Seeds grown in pasteurized compost, treated with feedings of compost tea, seldom die from damping-off, the fungal killer of young plants.

And if your plants or trees are already ailing, try nursing them back to health with compost water. Use this nutrient-rich solution at least once a week for sick plants. Pour it on bare spots in your lawn. You can also use it as a foliar spray by misting a strained solution directly onto plant leaves.

Adding compost to the bottom of planting holes assures that your transplants will get off to a good start

I follow the same practice when planting squash, pumpkins and cantaloupes in hills. I dig a hole instead of a furrow, scooping it out to a depth and width of 12 inches, then filling it almost to the top with compost. (If I'm short of compost I'll mix what I have with rich topsoil. Then I add several inches of soil to form a mound and plant the seeds. The compost provides a reservoir of nutrients for the young plants as they grow.

All my transplants get the same treatment. If I'm working with cabbage, broccoli, cauliflower or lettuce seedlings in the spring, for example, I'll use a trowel or bulb planter to dig a generous-size hole. Then, after filling the holes halfway with compost, I'll set the seedlings in, packing more humus around their root balls.

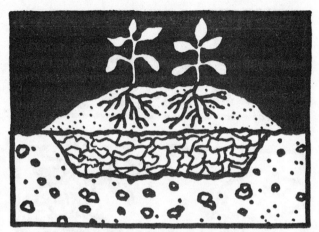

HILL-PLANTINGS: *For squash and other crops that benefit from planting in hills, dig a hole 12 inches deep and 12 inches wide, and fill with compost. Cover with soil to build up the mound, and plant.*

Tomatoes planted with compost also respond; they take off quickly and bear heavily until zapped by frost. Instead of digging a hole for tomato plants, however, I dig a 4-inch-deep furrow. After filling this with 2 inches of compost, I lay the tomato plant down in the furrow and bury the entire stem with topsoil and compost. I bend up the top 2 to 3 inches of the plant and hold it in a vertical position as I pack dirt around it for support.

At this point the tomato's stem lies horizontally 2 inches below the soil surface with perhaps 2 inches of leaf and stem showing above ground. Roots will soon form all along the buried stem, giving the plant an increased capacity for water and nutrient absorption.

I used to plant tomatoes vertically in compost-enriched holes until I realized the value of placing their stems horizontally close to the surface. Those 2 inches of humusy soil warm up rapidly in spring, much more quickly than would soil 6 to 8 inches down, packed around upright tomato stems. Fast-warming soil plus compost and active microorganisms means hardy, drought-proof, abundantly productive tomatoes.

Using compost this way—as an "oasis" of humus—has measurable benefits. The moist organic matter acts like a sponge; it is a water and plant food reservoir that can dole out food and water to your plants all season without much attention from you. True, it's a bit more work to excavate furrows and holes this way, but the results will pay you back many times over.

Mulching with compost is another excellent way to nourish your vegetable plants, shrubs and trees while controlling weeds, conserving moisture and improving soil structure. Mulch stays on the surface, of course, but earthworms will slowly drag organic matter down into the ground, leaving tunnels and nutrient-rich castings (earthworm manure). Mulching around plants with humus is actually sheet composting on a small scale. The practice will contribute significantly to soil improvement.

Don't mulch so early in the spring that you insulate the soil against warming. And, in areas where frost comes early, you'll want to remove the mulch in late summer. Organic matter piled around plants too late in the season can seal in some of the cold, making them more susceptible to frost damage and less open to the sun's warming rays.

As you mulch, it is important to remember that the finer the texture of the compost, the thinner the layer you'll need as a covering. Finished compost made of horse manure and peanut hulls, for example, would be as fine-textured as sawdust and a 3-inch layer would suffice as a mulch. But a coarser compost that is made with unshredded leaves, straw or hay would have to be applied in a layer at least 6 to 8 inches thick in order to produce the same effect.

PLANTING TOMATOES: *To ensure a strong root system for tomatoes (left), dig a 4-inch-deep furrow, and fill it with 2 inches of compost. Lay the tomato plant down in the furrow and bury the stem with topsoil and compost. Try to bend up the top 2 or 3 inches of stem and support with mounded soil. Roots will form along the entire length of the buried stem, increasing the plant's capacity for water and nutrient absorption.*

Using Compost in the Flower Garden: All types of flowers benefit from a generous application of screened compost. In the spring, when refurbishing your annual and perennial flower beds, work compost into the top 2 to 4 inches of soil. Use it also as a sidedressing for growing flowers, mixing it with the surface soil. Apply compost as a 1- to 2-inch-thick mulch to discourage weeds and conserve water.

SIDE-DRESSING FLOWER BEDS: *Compost can be used in your flower beds as well as in your vegetable garden. Place the compost between the rows of flower plants and work it into the soil about 1 inch deep.*

You can also use a mix of compost and vermiculite (described later in this chapter in the section titled Using Compost for House Plants and Seed-Starting) as a seeding medium for starting flowers. Or, if you seed flowers directly in the garden, use finely sifted compost to cover the seeds in the furrows.

Do you make it a practice to hill soil around your rose bushes to protect them over winter? Mix lots of compost in with the soil, and your roses will get a better start the following spring.

Using compost tea is another way to give your flowers some of the benefits of humus in liquid form. Build the large compost water barrel described in the previous chapter, or simply mix water and compost in a watering can. Let it steep for several hours at least (the

A mixture of equal parts of screened compost and vermiculite makes an excellent medium for starting flower seeds indoors

longer the better), then sprinkle generously around the plants.

Besides gently feeding your flowering plants, abundant doses of compost will keep the moisture content of flower beds high, a factor which discourages ants. There's also evidence that compost affects the colors of leaves, flowers and fruit. Plant coloration is determined by pigments found in chlorophyll, a substance made from chemicals like nitrogen, carbon dioxide and magnesium, found in the air and soil. Plants grown with ample, nutrient-rich humus may actually develop richer hues than plants grown solely with synthetic fertilizers or in poor soil.

Using Compost for Trees and Shrubs: You may not have enough finished compost to lavish as a mulch around all your trees and shrubs, so plan on sheet composting. For trees, dump the leaves, grass clippings, hay and other materials under the drip line, raking them into a ring that extends 2 feet from the trunk to a foot beyond the outermost branches. (Piling organic matter

PUTTING COMPOST AROUND TREES: *Place compost around each tree in a ring that extends 2 feet from the trunk to a foot beyond the outermost branches.*

up against the trunk offers a winter invitation to field mice and rabbits, who will burrow under it to feed on the bark.)

You can also recycle spoiled and rotted fruit by mulching with it beneath the trees it falls from. Covered with a 6-inch layer of clippings or dead leaves, rotted fruit won't attract flies or produce odors. Don't do this, however, if the fruit is diseased or badly infested with insects. Fruit in this condition should be added to a hot compost pile or burned.

A compost mulch applied to fruit trees has value beyond the nutrients it contributes. Because it keeps the soil cool, a heavy mulch discourages trees from blossoming too early in the spring, particularly during one of those freak thaws that's invariably followed by a killing frost.

Shrubs and bushes may be treated the same as trees. Work compost into the soil at their bases, or mulch with various types of organic matter.

Trees, shrubs and bushes of all kinds will also benefit from regular applications of compost tea.

Using Compost for House Plants and Seed-Starting: Humus derived from a hot composting process, one where all ingredients are subjected to core temperatures of 140° to 160°F, has been pasteurized naturally. Weed seeds have been destroyed, as have fly larvae and various disease organisms (such as those of damping-off, a disease that is the scourge of seedlings). Antibiotic substances produced by fungi during the composting process will also inhibit pathogens and parasites that might attack plants.

Thus, finished compost, screened and sifted, is an ideal seedling medium and potting soil. Because it hasn't been sterilized as commercial potting mixtures are, compost contains an abundance of beneficial microbial life and slow-release nutrients. Compost as a seeding medium encourages healthy germination and invigorates seedlings.

Don't wait until spring to assemble enough compost to fill your flats and pots. You'll want to have the compost on hand when you need it—in January, February or March, depending on where you live. Gather up an ample supply of pasteurized humus in the fall, after your garden chores have eased. Run the material through a screen of ¼-inch mesh hardware cloth and store it under cover in heavy-duty garbage bags or trash cans. (Save the coarse material the sifting produces. You can use it to line the bottom of flats and pots to ensure good drainage.) Be sure the compost is fully dry before sealing it up for the winter. Otherwise you'll be producing a bumper crop of fungus.

To use as a seed-starting mixture or potting soil for house plants, blend screened compost with an equal amount of vermiculite. This is a natural, micaceous mineral that's processed by heating to nearly 2,000°F, which pops it into puffy granules riddled with air cells. Thus treated, vermiculite is capable of holding air and several times its weight in water. It also contains some soluble potash and magnesium.

A blend of equal parts of vermiculite and compost is airy, moisture retentive but well drained, and well supplied with trace elements and growth-promoting organisms. (If, however, you prefer not to buy vermiculite, you may also use sand. Use round-grained river bottom or desert sand rather than sharp sand, which tends to compress more easily. A general-purpose potting soil may also be made with 2 parts garden loam, 1 part sand and 1 part compost.)

Another advantage of the vermiculite-compost mix is that you needn't add anything to balance the pH. Mixing in limestone when making potting soil is a tricky operation. It's easy to overdo the lime, causing an imbalance in the pH toward alkalinity. But finished compost is slightly acidic to neutral, while vermiculite is slightly alkaline, with a pH of 7.0 to 7.5; overall, a good balance is attained. Renew the potting medium once a year when practical to assure a well-drained, aerated medium. When you can't repot or prefer not to, add compost to window boxes and tubs by scratching it well into the surface several times a year. You can also custom-make compost from pine needles and oak leaves for acid-loving plants like azaleas.

Virtually all your house plants will benefit from occasional surface applications of screened compost. But while compost is an excellent plant food, the amount you'll use in flats and pots is small and frequently watered, so plan on feeding your plants some liquid

To make fine-textured compost for use in potting mixes, push compost through a screen of hardware cloth; the coarse material that's left can be used instead of pebbles to provide drainage in the bottom of pots

plant food regularly. Try using a blend of 1 tablespoon fish emulsion, 1 tablespoon liquid seaweed and 1 teaspoon blood meal in a gallon of water. Or use compost tea (see the instructions in the previous chapter for building a large compost tea container.) Feed seedlings every week to ten days, up until a week before you begin the hardening off process. House plants can be given feedings of compost tea twice monthly during their active growing season.

Screened compost also makes an excellent covering for newly sown seeds in hotbeds, cold frames, greenhouses and in the garden. Spread it evenly over the seeds, and keep it moist. It won't crust over and smother the emerging sprouts the way that heavy garden soil often does.

Grow-It

HOW COMPOST AFFECTS SOIL

The effect compost has on soil—any soil—is remarkable. No synthetic or chemical concoction or fertilizer whipped up in a laboratory can do what compost does. No matter what kind of shape your soil is in, whether it's hard-packed clay or superporous sand, liberal additions of humus can transform it into the rich loam all gardeners dream about.

Even if you live in a suburban development where bulldozers have scraped off the topsoil, leaving you to pick-axe your way through cementlike subsoil and rocks, digging in compost can help you build deep, crumbly, productive soil.

But perhaps you're lucky enough to have good soil that is loose and easily worked. Well, don't lean too long on your hoe handle counting your blessings. Even the best soil can be quickly worn out without regular additions of organic matter. That's why compost is the heart and soul of the organic method. With plenty of humus you can rebuild even the most savagely depleted soils, or keep already good soils in prime condition.

Why are compost and humus so important to a healthy garden? First of all, dirt isn't inert. Your garden's soil is an incredibly complex blend of mineral and organic matter, air, water and an astronomical population of soil life. Scoop up a teaspoonful of soil and you hold five billion microscopic organisms—yeasts, algae, fungi, viruses, protozoa and bacteria.

Look closely at a sample of soil, and you'll see a

> *Compost rebuilds poor and damaged soils in ways that no synthetic fertilizers can*

wriggling world of beetles, spiders, larvae, earthworms and many more creatures, all of whom make up the community you call a garden. But the major components of your soil—the ones that determine its physical structure and fertility—are the mineral and organic fractions.

Mineral matter is composed of particles of parent rock weathered and decomposed over many centuries. Organic matter, on the other hand, is decayed and living material like stems, roots, insect and animal carcasses, leaves and fecal droppings. Totally decomposed organic matter, as we've noted, is called humus. These two factors, the amount and type of organic matter in proportion to the size and type of the mineral particles, determine the texture and workability of a given soil—its tilth. To appreciate why this is so, let's take a closer look at the soil's mineral fraction.

All soils fall into three major categories—clay, sand and silt. Clay particles are the smallest, visible only under an electron microscope. Sand and salt particles are larger, from $\frac{1}{50}$ to $\frac{1}{2}$ inch in diameter. Most soils are mixtures of clay, sand and silt with their major characteristics determined by the dominant particle type.

Those infinitesimal clay particles, for instance, are wafer shaped. They flow together easily, forming a sticky mass that's starved for air and drains water poorly. Clay soils stay cold and wet in spring and become hard as bricks in dry weather. And when it does rain, much of the water rapidly runs off the sunbaked surface.

Yet, if you have difficulty working clay with a spade, imagine the difficulties plants have. Clay has ample nutrients held in solution, but roots have a terrible time fighting their way through the densely packed particles.

Loam, the ideal soil, contains all three types of soil particles — sand, silt and clay—in just the right proportions

Sandy soil tells the opposite tale. Coarse sand particles stay loose, admit air easily, allow plant roots to travel with relative ease and, because sand particles are unbound, cause water to drain away quickly—too quickly. Sandy soil lacks body, so precious nutrients are washed right out of the root zone, like water poured through a sieve full of marbles.

The ideal soil, called loam, falls between the extremes of dense clay and loose sand. Loam is a mixture of clay, sand and silt in just the proportions necessary to balance each particle's good features against another particle's limitations. Clay or sandy loams hold moisture without getting waterlogged. They drain well, but not so fast that nutrients are heavily lost through leaching.

But few gardeners have anything near an ideal soil, much less a rich loam. Most people are burdened with one of the soil extremes; their ground is either too heavy or too light. And even with a loam, many gardeners still complain that their plot never really produces that well. Something seems to be missing. That something is organic matter and humus.

Soil structure begins to improve the very first time you apply compost

Compost and Soil Structure

Most soils contain some organic matter, but the actual amount varies dramatically according to the location and condition of the ground. A well-worked garden or farm whose owners have been negligent about returning crop residues, compost or manure to the earth may only have a 1 percent supply of organic matter in the soil. In contrast, early North American farmers sunk their plows into virgin prairie containing 7 to 10 percent organic matter in the top 12 inches of soil.

Humus is vitally important to soil health because of its effect on the physical condition of the mineral fraction. Let's assume you have a clay soil with all the unfortunate features of that heavy medium. In this case, when you begin digging in compost, the grains of humus wedge themselves between the flat clay particles, thereby opening the mass, creating porosity, admitting air and allowing water to drain.

Perhaps you have a sandy soil. Add humus, and the beneficial effects will be similar. The organic particles will give the unbound sand grains some body and absorbency. Your excessively loose soil will become more like a blotter, holding water and nutrients in place.

Of course, none of this happens overnight. You can't just run out, dump on a one-shot application of compost and expect dramatic improvements. You must add compost regularly and heavily while avoiding the cardinal sin of compacting the soil excessively. Yet, given that you use compost liberally, you will see some changes, even in a single season.

EFFECT OF HUMUS ON CLAY SOILS: *The tiny, wafer-shaped clay particles fit tightly together, making it difficult for roots and water to penetrate (left). With the addition of humus, the mass of clay is opened up, creating greater porosity and allowing water and air to enter more freely (right).*

ADDING HUMUS TO SANDY SOIL: *Water, along with valuable nutrients, passes quickly through the loosely structured soil composed of many large sand particles (left). When humus is worked into the soil, the sand particles gain body and absorbency, increasing their ability to hold water and nutrients for plant use (right).*

Your soil's crumb structure will begin to improve with the first spreading or digging in of compost. Have you ever looked closely at really good garden soil? The dirt forms into specks that look like coffee grounds. This is a natural and desired phenomenon in humus-rich soils. The various chemicals released by humus act as a glue or slime, that coats mineral particles and binds them together into loose but definite aggregates or granules.

This crumbly texture is an ideal environment for plant and soil life. The wedging and binding effect of humus particles and humic acids encourages the freer passage of air and water. Also, plant roots and soil organisms move more easily through granulated earth as they search for nourishment. A good crumb structure is also important because microscopic root hairs must extract their food from nutrients held in a thin film of water-coating soil particles.

Heavy clay impedes this process by locking up nutrients both physically and chemically. With excessively loose soil, on the other hand, nutrients quickly wash out of the root zone. However, by regularly adding compost to your garden, you exert an equalizing influence. Using compost balances soil extremes by creating countless tiny crumbs of humus-coated mineral matter that hold water and plant food in reserve.

COMPOST EXTENDS
THE GROWING SEASON

Did you know that using lots of compost in your garden can give you a longer growing season? You can start earlier in the spring and keep harvesting food longer into the early winter. Compost darkens your soil which, in turn, causes it to be a better solar collector. Dark surfaces absorb heat more effectively than pale hues, so a humusy soil will naturally warm up sooner and stay warm longer than light-colored land.

The aeration properties of humus also contribute to this effect by keeping soil porous and moist. Heavy, wet soils always stay cooler longer into the spring than sandy or humus-rich earth.

Those crumbs also hold air. We've discussed the importance of oxygen in the compost pile, but for optimum health your garden soil should be equally aerobic. Compacted or waterlogged soils have little space for oxygen, creating anaerobic conditions that slow microbial activity, decrease the absorption of water and minerals and retard the growth of plant roots and tops. These conditions may even cause the formation of certain inorganic compounds toxic to plant development.

Gardeners don't often think of air as a nutrient, but its presence in the soil is all-important. Without sufficient oxygen, the little humus that an air-starved soil might contain becomes biologically inactive; the soil's nitrogen content decreases; the pH rises into the alkaline range; and the overall content of organic matter drops.

Many soil processes are also dependent on proper aeration. Various minerals necessary for plant development are changed into forms that are useful to plants only in the presence of oxygen. Sulfur is converted to sulfur dioxide, carbon to carbon dioxide and ammonia to nitrate by an oxidative process. So a poorly aerated soil may significantly limit the amount and type of minerals available to plants.

Plenty of air also stimulates the activity of aerobic microbial life. We've seen the importance of certain soil-dwelling bacteria and fungi in the composting process. These and other microbial life forms play a critical role in the soil at large: in the conversion of nitrogen and other minerals into forms absorbable by roots, in the decomposition of organic matter, and in the creation of natural antibiotic substances.

A porous soil literally breathes; it exchanges gases with the atmosphere. Aboveground, leaves take in carbon dioxide and release oxygen. The opposite occurs beneath the surface. Roots absorb oxygen and give off carbon dioxide. But the decomposition of organic matter also releases carbon dioxide, so unless a soil is permeable, roots and microbes will starve for oxygen while suffering from an overload of carbon dioxide.

But, fortunately, it's not difficult to pump air into your soil. Humus-rich earth is automatically well aerated, honeycombed with pockets of air.

Compost as Plant Food

But beyond its effect on the mechanics of soil structure, just how good is compost as a plant food? Organic gardeners will tell you that it can't be beat. However, the clerk in your local garden shop will probably disagree, arguing that "you can't grow good vegetables without putting on real fertilizer." The not-so-subtle implication: that compost is somehow inferior to a sack of the latest petrochemical brew.

Compost is a gentle, balanced plant food that delivers nutrients gradually over a period of time—just the way plants need them

While it's true that compost, no matter how carefully made, doesn't have the immediate chemical punch of synthetic fertilizers, this characteristic is actually a strength rather than a weakness. The "power" of synthetic fertilizers can (and does) actually harm our soils, wreak havoc on our rivers and streams and keep us dependent on superexpensive oil and natural gas.

Compost is simple, free, abundant and naturally effective. Maybe that's why it seems too good to be true. Yet examine the way plants nourish themselves. Through photosynthesis, plants use sunlight falling on their leaves to convert air and water into their basic food, a sugar compounded of carbon, hydrogen and oxygen. But plants need more than sunshine; they also need a balanced diet of minerals—phosphorus, potassium, nitrogen and sulfur (the macronutrients) in large amounts; magnesium, chlorine, boron and probably sodium (the micronutrients) in small amounts; and copper, zinc, molybdenum and manganese (the trace elements) in minute amounts.

The Process of Cation Exchange: Carbon, hydrogen and some nitrogen are available to plants from the atmosphere, but the majority of necessary minerals must be derived from the soil, absorbed by the roots as submicroscopic particles. Various minerals are found in the soil as cations, or positively charged molecules. Molecules of humus and clay, however, are anions; they are negatively charged. Because opposites attract, cations are naturally attracted to humus and clay anions and will attach themselves like magnets, thus being

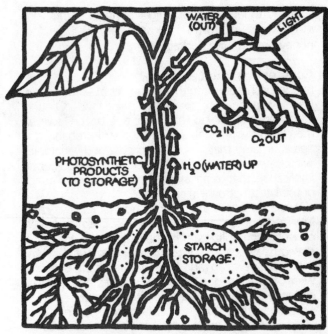

PHOTOSYNTHESIS: *During photosynthesis green plants convert solar energy into chemical energy. Water is absorbed through the roots and translocated up the stem to the leaves through capillary action. In the presence of sunlight, carbon dioxide, which is admitted through the stomates in the leaves, and water are transformed into carbohydrates. Excess water and oxygen are liberated into the atmosphere and the carbohydrates move down the stem for storage in the roots.*

held in the soil and available to roots. When plant roots make use of the minerals by absorbing them, the process of "cation exchange" has taken place. Minerals found as cations include potassium, magnesium, calcium, ammonium (a nitrogen form found in small amounts in soil), copper, iron and sodium.

Now imagine a root hair growing through the soil in search of nutrients. When it makes contact with a soil particle laden with some necessary cations—magnesium, for example—the root releases positively

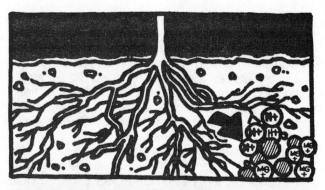

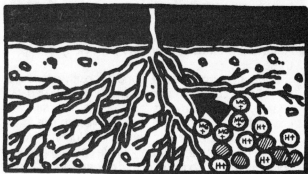

CATION EXCHANGE: *When nutrient-seeking roots come in contact with soil particles with necessary cations, such as magnesium in this case, the bound hydrogen cations (top) are released and exchanged for an equal amount of magnesium cations (bottom). The mineral ions are then absorbed into the roots to be utilized by the plant.*

charged hydrogen ions. These knock loose an equal amount of magnesium cations. The exchange occurs as hydrogen ions attach themselves to the soil particles while the magnesium cations move over to the root to be absorbed into the plant's system.

The capacity of a soil to exchange cations is the best measurement of its fertility. Plants, like people, are healthy and productive in direct relation to their ability to absorb and utilize nutrients. And this is where the importance and indispensable qualities of compost become most apparent.

A soil's fertility is measured by its ability to exchange cations, and compost improves this ability — its most important contribution to plant health

Let's go back to the way nutrient cations attach themselves to soil particles. Obviously the more cations fixed to a given soil particle, the better, since there would be that much more mineral food held in the soil and available for absorption by plants. But the attraction and attachment of cations to soil depends largely on the surface area of a particular soil particle. The more surface area it has, the more places there are for cations to attach themselves.

Humus particles have more surface area than clay, so soil rich in organic matter will always have a greater exchange capability than humus-poor soil—no matter how much synthetic fertilizer you pour on. (Sand and silt have the lowest cation exchange capacity since their particles are unable to hold or swap nutrients. Adequate humus is therefore especially crucial in these soils.)

But not all nutrients are found as positively charged ions. Some occur as anions, which have a negative charge. These nutrients are repelled by similarly charged soil particles and aren't subject to cation exchange. Anions must be taken up in solution by roots. Nitrogen (as nitrate), phosphorus (as phosphate) and compounds of carbon, sulfur and chlorine are examples of water-soluble anions. Phosphate, however, can bind itself to the soil; nitrogen cannot. Nitrogen is easily leached out by rain and erosion, a major problem when gardeners and farmers rely on synthetic fertilizers instead of building up the soil's humus content.

Providing Balanced Nutrition: Excess nitrogen can flow into groundwater, streams and rivers. There it stimulates the rapid, unchecked growth of algae, which can expand into a green blanket capable of choking open waters into biological death. Compost, even when used in huge amounts, presents no such problems. Because humus has such outstanding natural moisture retention, it's able to hold water-soluble nutrients in place, slowing their loss by leaching or erosion.

Nor can the nitrogen found in compost be flooded into the ecosystem, as is the case with commercial fertilizers. Fully 35 percent of the synthetic nitrogen and 15 to 20 percent of the phosphorus and potassium applied as commercial fertilizers are lost because they wash away after spreading. Gardeners and farmers compound this problem by throwing more fertilizer on their soils than plants can immediately assimilate. These chemical salts, unlike compost, are immediately soluble. But humus is a storehouse of all the nutrients needed by plants. It releases its elements slowly to feed crops gradually over the seasons.

Composted manure, for example, discharges 50 percent of its nutrients during the first season, less each year thereafter. This means that continuous applications of compost actually build a reserve of plant foods—a true soil bank. Humusy soil could, in fact, provide crops with sustenance for several seasons even if no further compost was added.

You can't say that about synthetic fertilizers. They're a one-shot application, an artificial addition, whereas compost is a natural soil component. Commercial fertilizers do nothing to build the soil's structure or tilth. They also vanish downstream or into the atmosphere after a single growing season, and they must be reapplied annually at an ever increasing cost.

The only difference between composting and the natural process it imitates is the amount of time it takes; while you can revitalize bad soil in just a few years with compost, nature takes 100 years to do the same thing

But when you add compost to your garden, you're basically carrying on nature's ancient soil-building program, the same process that gave us the forests and the deep soil of the prairies. The only difference between your efforts to build the humus content and what happens naturally is that conscientious composting can reclaim poor or denuded soil in several years, while nature might take a century or more to accomplish the same thing.

Commercial fertilizers also supply a narrow range of nutrients, mainly just nitrogen, phosphorus and potash. But because a greater variety of ingredients is used to make compost, more known and unknown nutrients and substances are found in the end product, though in a less concentrated and volatile form. Humus feeds the entire soil community, dispensing its nutrients through a natural timed-release mechanism.

Soil-dwelling microbes that help free the various chemicals increase their activity as the soil warms. Vital substances and minerals are made available to roots gradually, in tandem with plant growth. Seedlings get small amounts of nutrients in spring and larger amounts as the soil grows warmer and the season progresses.

So there's little danger of overfeeding or poisoning crops with compost. Humus, particularly when composed of a variety of materials, usually contains balanced amounts of plant foods in the forms that are most usable to plants.

Compost can also help neutralize toxins in the soil. For example, excess aluminum found naturally in the soil may create problems as it stops plants from absorbing phosphorus. But plenty of actively decomposing organic matter in soil produces humic acids that combine with aluminum and bind it into a form unavailable to roots. The same acids also help plants to absorb the available phosphorus more efficiently. This is doubly important, because studies have shown that plants with access to adequate amounts of phosphorus are less likely to take up toxic, heavy metals like cadmium.

Compost Helps Balance pH

Plant uptake of heavy metals is also influenced by soil pH and its acidity or alkalinity. Crops accumulate fewer heavy metals as the soil nears neutral, between 6.5 and 7.0 on the pH scale. Here again, abundant humus can exert a profoundly beneficial effect on soil by balancing pH extremes. This is important not only because of the problem of heavy metals but because pH directly affects how plants take up nutrients. Soils that are excessively acid or alkaline will produce stunted or poor quality plants and a limited harvest.

The letters pH stand for "potential hydrogen," or "power of hydrogen." When we measure pH, we're actually assessing the intensity of hydrogen in the soil water. The water molecule is composed of two parts hydrogen and one part oxygen. Reacting with mineral and organic compounds in the soil, this molecule splits into two parts, a positively charged ion of hydrogen (H+) and a negatively charged oxygen-hydrogen ion (OH−). The relative proportions of these particles in a given soil determine its acidity or alkalinity.

Acid soil is overloaded with H+ ions, while alkaline soil contains more OH− particles. Neutral soils, ideal for vegetable growing, have an equal amount of each. In acid soil, the H+ ions displace important nutrients like calcium, magnesium and potassium, bumping them off soil particles and making them less available to plant roots through cation exchange. Rain (even the old-fashioned, nonacid type) accentuates this process as it seeps through acidic organic matter, picking up more H+ ions and depositing them on soil particles. Without adjustment by the gardener, the soil will grow increasingly acid as H+ ions replace nutrients.

The hydroxyl ion (OH−) predominates in alkaline areas. Alkaline soils contain an abundance of base minerals—calcium, magnesium and potassium—but these (plus copper, iron, manganese and others) are chemically bound to the OH− ion and unavailable to roots.

Think of soil as a kitchen and plant roots as proverbial hungry travelers. In acid soil the kitchen is filled with nonfood H+ ions and the roots can't get a decent meal. In alkaline soil the kitchen is packed with nutrients but the door is locked tight. Therefore, regardless of whether soil is too acid or too alkaline, the consequences to plants are the same: poor nutrition and limited development.

Balanced pH is important for a healthy garden; soil that is too acid or too alkaline impedes the flow of nutrients to plants

Nor is this the only problem caused by an unbalanced pH. Overacidity causes aluminum, iron and manganese to become highly available to roots, sometimes in toxic quantities. At the other extreme, alkaline soils can suffer a buildup of mineral salts strong enough to inhibit much plant life of any kind.

You can determine your garden's pH by testing a soil sample with one of the litmus paper or solution test kits sold in garden shops. You can get a more accurate assessment by sending a soil sample to your local agriculture extension office. Its tests, conducted by the nearest agriculture school, are precise and done at little or no cost.

Whatever testing method you use will show acidity and alkalinity expressed on a scale of 1 to 14, with 7 being neutral. Everything below 7 is increasingly acidic; everything above is increasingly alkaline. A peat bog might have a pH of 3, a desert 10 to 11. Most vegetables can adapt to a range of pH levels, but a slightly acid to neutral soil rich in humus is ideal.

Aside from satisfying the pH needs of most vegetables, moderately acid soil is also the most suitable environment for those all-important soil bacteria responsible for, among other things, converting atmospheric nitrogen into a form absorbable by roots and for rapidly transforming raw organic matter into humus. Nonorganic gardeners, in fact, can pour on bags of expensive fertilizer to no avail if the soil pH is skewed. Nitrogen in the form of urea and ammonia salts is useless to plants until those nitrifying bacteria convert it to nitrates—something they can't do if the pH is very far off from neutral.

Adjusting Your Soil's pH: Once you have a pH reading you can begin balancing your soil. If the garden area is excessively alkaline, dig in plenty of acidic compost made from oak leaves and pine needles, peat moss, apple pomace, cottonseed meal and hardwood sawdust.

If your soil is acidic, add lime and generous spreadings of compost and organic matter. Use natural ground or pulverized limestone, either calcic or dolomitic. Ground lime fine enough to pass through a 60 to 100 mesh (look for this information on the bag) is nontoxic and nonburning, and it will gradually weather and dissolve in the soil. Lime also causes clay particles to form crumbs, helps sand grains to bind more closely and interacts with humus, stimulating the production of natural "glues" that coat soil granules and improve tilth.

You can also use wood ashes to neutralize acidity. Containing potassium, calcium and phosphoric acid (the amounts vary according to the type of wood burned), wood ashes are more soluble than limestone and should be applied less heavily (about half as much) and more frequently (at least annually). Other naturally alkaline soil conditioners include pulverized marble (unburned), marl (a slow-release lime-clay sediment), and ground oyster shells.

How much lime should you apply? There are rules of thumb, but every soil is different. Two gardens with the same pH won't necessarily have the same lime requirement. Wet areas with sandy soil, for example, need more frequent applications of lime than dry gardens with heavy soil. But heavy clay in general needs more lime applied at one time. The chart How Much Lime to Add provides a rough liming guide, but check with your extension service for more exact local soil information.

Test your soil in early spring or fall, then apply lime to freshly cultivated ground, working it into the top 3 to 4 inches. Wearing a dust mask or respirator, broadcast the lime by hand or apply it with a spreader.

HOW MUCH LIME TO ADD

To raise soil pH by one unit, add the following amounts of ground limestone or dolomitic lime per 100 square feet:

Soil Type	Amount to Add
Light Soil	2½ pounds ground lime or 2 pounds dolomite
Heavy Soil	6 pounds ground lime or 5½ pounds dolomite

Do this on a windless day. Coverage should look like a moderate dusting of snow. You can't change acid soil to neutral overnight, so don't overlime.

Wait at least a month, then retest the pH. Add lime or wood ashes regularly until the pH is only slightly acid. Check your pH at least annually, more often (spring, midseason and fall) if you wish. Some gardens need yearly liming, while others do well with applications only every few years.

Compost made from a variety of materials can buffer soil pH

Most important of all, keep adding plenty of compost made from mixed materials such as manure, grass clippings, dead leaves and kitchen scraps—the more variety the better. Humus will not only dramatically improve the soil's structure but will also exert a buffering effect on the pH. As mixed organic materials rot, the decomposition process releases roughly equal amounts of acid and alkaline compounds. This helps stabilize soil pH at near-neutral levels.

Even more significant is the fact that the presence of ample humus tends to increase a plant's tolerance for pH differences. Thus a well-composted garden, aside from all its other virtues, will probably have plants better able to adapt to a wide range of environmental factors, including variations in soil acidity and alkalinity.

Compost and Earthworms

Another of compost's important contributions is its encouragement of the soil's earthworm population. Earthworms are an asset in cool, long-standing compost piles, where they help break down organic matter, but the worms' chief benefits are to the garden proper. In fact, the absence of worm activity in the garden is often an indication of poor soil that is tightly compacted and lacking in humus.

Earthworms are most active in the top 6 inches of soil, but they may burrow as deep as 6 feet, pulling organic matter down with them and dragging subsoil back up to the surface on their return. Aristotle called earthworms "the earth's intestines," and their churning of the soil does mimic digestion on a grand scale.

Each square foot of reasonably good garden soil harbors about two dozen worms collectively able to digest 1,000 pounds of soil annually. (Each worm eats its own weight in soil and organic matter daily.) The amount of mineral rich subsoil worms pull upward is also significant. Worms living in a single acre of ground bring up about 20 tons of subsoil each year.

They also leave prodigious amounts of excreta, called "castings." As the blind, toothless worms ingest particles of organic and mineral matter, their rudimentary digestive systems extract the food value, combining the residue with secretions of calcium carbonate and gut mucus. Castings are expelled as granular pellets, a superb soil conditioner. A healthy worm population can leave more than 50 tons of castings annually per acre.

Besides the profound effects castings have on soil structure, the myriad tunnels worms leave also make significant contributions to aeration and water drainage and provide pathways for roots to travel in their search for nutrients and water. Earthworm activity may also affect soil pH, bringing acid and alkaline soils within the neutral range.

Even in death the earthworm makes a final important

EARTHWORMS IN THE GARDEN: *Earthworms are welcome occupants of any gardener's soil. In the course of their life processes, the worms in your garden can digest thousands of pounds of soil and pull up tons of subsoil laden with minerals. Their castings improve soil conditions, and the tunnels they produce in their movements open up compact soils, improving aeration and water drainage.*

contribution by adding its decaying body to the soil's humus content. Worms live only a year or two at most, so the typical life cycle of two dozen worms per square foot adds 1,100 pounds of carcasses per acre annually.

All the soil improvements wrought by the normal behavior of earthworms would cost a fortune if they had to be performed by human or machine power. But you needn't pay a penny for the labors of "nature's plowmen." Just avoid using chemical fertilizers and pesticides, some of which kill worms on contact. And don't compress your soil with heavy equipment or excessive foot traffic. Instead, add plenty of worm food compost and mulch.

GATHERING COMPOST MATERIALS

Y ou've probably noticed the phrase "compost from a variety of materials" several times in this book. There's an important reason for stressing variety in the ingredients you choose to make compost. Gardening, particularly vegetable production, makes intense demands on the soil. You'll want to replace all the known and unknown nutrients and growth stimulants your crops take up. Making humus from as many sources as possible is an effective way to do this.

The greater the variety of organic matter you convert to humus, the richer the bounty of nutrients and trace elements you'll return to the soil. Fortunately, you don't have to go far for compostable ingredients. Consider what goes on right in your community. People are probably throwing away, burning or burying the very materials that might be used to build a deep, crumbly soil.

Compost made from a variety of materials supplies a broader range of major nutrients and trace elements to your garden soil than do many commercial fertilizer preparations

Where to Get Compost Materials

Start with your own home and yard. The rule for compostables is, with few exceptions, that everything organic—whatever has lived or been part of a living thing—is fair game for the heap. (We'll get to those exceptions later in this chapter.) This includes all wastes from your yard and garden; kitchen scraps and spoiled foods; hair clippings from the family and the pet dogs; even dust from your vacuum cleaner. Think of all the things you throw out or discard. Might they be turned into humus?

A story appeared some years ago about an avid

organic gardener who accidently cut his finger while working in the kitchen. "Get me a Band-Aid!" he shouted as he ran for the back door. His wife got the bandage and antiseptic but where was he going? Then she saw and laughed: he was standing over his compost pile, letting his sliced finger bleed onto the heap. "It shouldn't go to waste," he said, laughing at himself.

You needn't go quite that far in making contributions to your compost pile, but once you've exhausted the possibilities around your home you'll want to check the Yellow Pages for sources of organic castoffs in your community. You may have to pay for some of this stuff, but consider it a wise investment if the fee is nominal. Compost and good soil pay unlimited dividends.

It is still possible to get compost materials free for the hauling from many places

Here's a partial list of places to contact for compost materials:

Stables and feedlots: These are your best sources of manure, though you may have to get in line with other gardeners. Still, the animals produce daily all year, so there's generally enough manure for everyone if you're patient.

Some police departments, forestry and park services use mounted patrols and have their own stables. They are usually willing to let gardeners come at a set time to haul away manure.

Racetracks produce enormous amounts of manure and have it hauled off, usually by commercial mushroom growers. But you may be able to strike a deal with an individual horse owner or trainer for a share, especially if you're willing to clean the stable and load the manure yourself.

Also try amusement and city parks with pony rings. And when the circus comes to town, get in line for the elephant manure!

Farms and orchards: A drive through the countryside or a few phone calls may produce truckloads of organic wastes for your garden. Don't expect much waste from organic farms, however. The owners will likely be turning all their organic matter back into the soil. But other operations may be glad to let you haul off as much materials as you want. Consider renting or borrowing a truck before you go.

Materials to ask about include prunings or shredded material from orchards, whey from dairy operations, spent mushroom soil (but ask about their use of agricultural chemicals before bringing the stuff home), spoiled hay, rotten fruit, feathers, eggshells, corn silage, barnyard wastes and manure of all kinds.

City departments: What does your town do with the leaves and lawn clippings its sanitation workers pick up? Does your town clear its streams, lakes and ponds of aquatic weeds? What happens to this material? Are the chips from municipal tree trimming and brush cutting operations available to citizens? Some enlightened communities compost all their wastes and provide free humus to their taxpayers. A phone call may be all it takes to answer these questions to your benefit.

Mills and factories: Commercial operations produce tons of organic matter that often goes to the nearest landfill. For the most accurate information about these materials, ask your questions by starting at the top. Call the company president's office and work your way down the chain of command. This will save time. Stopping by or calling the loading dock means you have to work backward, getting permission and clearances and making endless explanations of just why you want the stuff in the first place. The public information or public relations office, if the company has one, may also help you.

Here are some of the materials available from processors: apple pomace from cider mills, cannery wastes of all kinds, shredded bark, sawdust and wood shavings from lumber mills and carpentry shops, botanical drug wastes from pharmaceutical firms, cement dust, cocoa bean hulls, coffee chaff from coffee wholesalers, cottonseed meal, excelsior from receiving or shipping departments, felt and wool wastes from clothing manufacturers, agricultural frit from glass factories, grape pomace from wineries, spent hops from breweries, granite dust from cutting operations, leather dust, lignin from paper mills, spoiled meal from flour mills, peanut hulls, slag from steel mills, spice marc (spent) from spice packers, tanbark from tanneries and tankage from meat processing plants and slaughterhouses.

Retail shops: Small shopkeepers may be glad to see you come in to haul off what they usually pay to have removed: vegetable and fish scraps from supermarkets and food stores, hair from barbers and salons, pet hair from poodle parlors, kitchen scraps from restaurants, spoiled breadstuffs from bakeries, excelsior from gift shops (used for packing breakables), plant wastes from florists and sawdust from cabinetmakers and lumberyards.

Waterways and seashores: Get permission if necessary to harvest marsh grass and seaweed from ocean and bay beaches and estuaries. Or gather these materials after a storm when they're washed up on the beach. Many streams, lakes and ponds in your community may be choked with algae and other aquatic plants (caused, perhaps, by the overuse of commercial fertilizers). Your cleaning up and hauling off this nuisance may be a real service to land owners and municipal authorities. But check with property owners, park authorities and environmental groups before you begin cutting, raking and loading. What seems like useless plants to you may actually serve an important ecological function.

Be on the lookout for materials unique to your area. If you live in New England, check for wastes from maple syrup production, wood wastes, wool and felt scraps from manufacturers and leather scraps and dust from shoe companies. Northeastern residents near the seacoast should be able to acquire large amounts of seaweed, greensand and fish scraps.

Gardeners in the Southwest can search for cannery wastes, mesquite, olive residue, volcanic rock, grape seeds and pomace from wineries and citrus pulp.

Those in the South should look for cotton gin trash, Spanish moss, peanut hulls and peanut shell ashes, snuff wastes, tung-oil pomace, sugarcane trash, molasses residue, castor pomace, tobacco stems, rice hulls and water hyacinth plants.

Organic gardeners can serve an important role in collecting such "wastes" that might otherwise plague the community and the local environment by ending up as pollutants. But besides lifting a small part of the burden on your fellow taxpayers, you'll be functioning as an agent of change. People will express surprise and curiosity at your collection and composting of what

Take advantage of your geographic location and the industries in your area when searching for compost materials; each region has its own special sources

103

they had previously considered useless stuff. Your recycling and humus making will act as a reminder that garbage and organic trash are really <u>resources</u>, not problems, if we use our collective imaginations and practice self-reliance.

When supplemental fertilizers like rock powders are added to the compost heap rather than applied directly to soil, their nutrients are made more readily available to plants

Additional Materials: There are lots of ingredients you can add to boost the nutrient content of your finished compost. Many classic composting techniques suggest adding sprinklings of various rock powders as you build the layers of the heap. Granite dust, phosphate rock, greensand and others are all valuable for their minerals, though their addition to the pile doesn't actually enhance or speed up the composting process.

What does happen is that the nutrients contained in these supplemental materials are broken down by the humification process, attacked by microbes and humic acids and rendered more available to plant roots. This alone makes their addition to a working compost heap valuable, because your finished humus will be far more potent than otherwise.

Check your local garden centers and mail-order sources for a variety of soil amendments: basalt rock powder, bagged and dried manure, dried blood, bone meal, cottonseed meal, greensand marl, horn and hoof meal, tobacco stems, powdered kelp, peat moss and granite meal.

The only drawback to these ingredients is their cost. Some, like dried blood, are almost prohibitive to purchase in large amounts. Gardeners must decide on the more economical course—whether to add the materials to the compost heap or use them directly around plants as sidedressings.

What Not to Use in a Compost Pile
Everything of an organic nature will compost, but not everything belongs in your compost pile. Some materials are questionable, some should be used in moderate amounts, and some should be avoided altogether. Remember also that the materials in an efficient compost heap (whether fast or slow) should be mixed to balance their moisture content. So even if you're lucky enough to drive home with a load of spent hops from a brewery, you still have to use caution. That soggy mass (like

straight cow manure without bedding) can't be composted by itself—at least not without generating a monumental stench. All dense, wet materials must be used in conjunction with absorbent matter like hay, straw, sawdust, dead leaves or wood chips.

A Note on Using Lime in the Compost Pile

Many gardening books and gardeners will tell you to add lime as you build the layers of your compost heap. Even the classic Indore method suggests that a dusting of lime be added to successive layers of the pile to offset the acidity of leaves and similar acidic materials. Adding lime also tends to improve the physical condition and workability of composting materials.

But there's good reason to add lime directly on your garden soil rather than on the compost heap to balance pH. Why? Because lime added to raw, decomposing matter causes a chemical reaction that promotes the loss of nitrogen by creating ammonia gas. Besides this waste of a valuable nutrient, lime simply isn't necessary in the composting process.

As was explained in the text, a well-made compost pile comprised of mixed ingredients may vary in pH during the active stages of decomposition, but the mass will then settle naturally to a neutral pH or nearly so (6.5 to 7.0) when the decay process is completed. So lime your garden soil regularly, but not your compost pile.

Should you use human feces in the compost heap? While farmers and gardeners have for centuries used their own wastes as fertilizer, it's best to avoid this material unless you possess the specialized knowledge, equipment and experience necessary for its safe disposition. Disease organisms are easily spread through contact with human fecal matter.

To render such material safe for use on edible fruits and vegetables, it must be either thoroughly decomposed in a carefully tended, high-heat compost pile or allowed to decay very slowly—in the chamber of a composting toilet, for example. (Human urine from healthy individuals, however, is sterile, safe and valuable to use in compost and garden. See its listing under A Guide to Compost Materials found later in this chapter.)

Avoid the following materials, which resist decomposition unless you're able to shred or chop them into chips: chunks of wood or lumber, large prunings, brush, cornstalks or sunflower stalks, large amounts of pine needles, eucalyptus leaves, clam shells and oyster shells, rags, paper and heavy cardboard.

It's OK to use paper in the compost heap, but don't use the Sunday comics section — those colored inks contain cadmium and lead

Paper, shredded and in moderate amounts, can be useful in composting because it provides absorbency and bulk. It contains few nutrients, however. Avoid colored paper or glossy magazine stock. Ordinary black-and-white newsprint is safe to use, but colored inks and glossy paper contain significant amounts of cadmium and other heavy metals that may leach into your compost and soil.

Highly acid materials—pine needles and oak leaves, for example—used alone or unbalanced by neutral or alkaline ingredients will produce an acidic humus. This is fine if you wish to add it to alkaline soil or to acid-loving plants like blueberries or azaleas, but it is a curse if your soil is already acidic. Use a wide variety of compostables unless you specifically want acidic humus.

Don't try to compost grease, oil or large amounts of meat, fish or poultry scraps. These materials take a long time to decay, go anaerobic easily and attract animal and insect scavengers. You can still use them for soil building, but only if you bury them in a little-used part of the garden. They take a long time to decompose even when buried, though, and they must be placed at least 6 inches under the surface to discourage scavengers.

Be careful harvesting weeds and grass along roadsides where highway departments may have sprayed with herbicides. Heavily traveled roads are also poor places to forage for compostables (or wild foods) because toxic particles from exhaust fumes settle on plant leaves.

Don't use coal ashes in the compost pile. It's true that coal wastes contain soluble sulfur and iron, but the amounts found in some types of coal can be toxic to soil and plant life. Ashes from some soft coals may contain up to 10 percent sulfur trioxide which, when mixed with water, produces sulfuric acid—hardly a beneficial addition to your compost pile or soil.

Also, don't be tempted to use incinerator wastes in the compost heap or garden. Many gardeners can get these ashes from apartment house incinerators, but the risk involved doesn't justify their use. All kinds of things get tossed into incinerators—everything from old batteries laden with mercury, zinc and cadmium to various sorts of plastics. The heavy metal residues in the ashes may be harmful to your soil and plants.

A Guide to Compost Materials

Alfalfa: This is a perennial herbaceous legume grown as livestock feed and as a superior green manure or cover crop. Alfalfa grows almost everywhere in the United States and is widely available as hay or dehydrated feed pellets. Its nitrogen content and absorbency make it an excellent addition to the compost pile.

Alfalfa's carbon/nitrogen ratio is 12 to 1, so mixing it with equal parts of leaves or fruit wastes will yield that ideal C/N ratio of 25 or 30 to 1. Good alfalfa hay is expensive, however. Ask farmers and feed stores for rotted or spoiled bales unsuitable as animal feed.

Apple pomace: Anyone who presses his or her own apple cider produces heaps of this sweet pulp. Yellow jackets, hornets and bees love to zero in on the residues, so it's best to get the pomace into a working compost heap as soon as possible. Fresh pomace is wet and heavy and must be well mixed with dry leaves, hay or other absorbent matter.

While low in nitrogen (only one-fifth of 1 percent), it does contain valuable amounts of phosphoric acid and potash. If you haul pomace in from commercial presses, however, do investigate their source and the use of pesticides. Apple skins may contain residues of metallic sprays, especially if the sprays are used heavily. If you

If you want to use commercially produced fruit or vegetable wastes for composting, inquire first about how heavily the crops were sprayed with pesticides

use pomace in large amounts, these residues could conceivably build up toxic elements in your soil.

Bagasse: Deep South gardeners will have access to this valuable plant residue of sugarcane processing. (See the Sugar wastes entry later in this section.)

Banana residues: The skins and stalks of this tropical fruit contain abundant amounts of phosphoric acid and potash. Banana skins also decompose rapidly, a sign that the microbes of decay are well supplied with nitrogen. Banana skins are usually a staple in kitchen scraps, and their use in a compost heap will guarantee lots of bacterial activity. Get the skins incorporated into the core of the pile, or cover quickly with organic matter to avoid attracting flies.

Basic slag: This is an industrial by-product formed when iron ore is smelted to make pig iron. The smelting process uses large amounts of limestone and dolomite that combine with impurities in the ore, rising as a sludge that coats the surface of the molten metal. Skimmed off, cooled and hardened, the resultant slag contains numerous minerals also found in the soil—lime, magnesium, silicon, aluminum, manganese, sulfur and iron. It also contains trace elements of boron, chromium, copper, molybdenum, potassium, sodium, strontium, tin, titanium, vanadium, zinc and zirconium. The exact percentage of these minerals depends on variations in the smelting process.

Packaged slag has been pulverized into a fine black powder so it can be used as a soil-builder in gardening and farming. The material is alkaline and is popular as a liming agent. In fact, tests show that slag is actually better for this purpose than lime because of its greater store of minerals.

Slag can be applied liberally to soil or compost heap with no fear of overuse. It won't burn plants or roots. Beans, peas, clover, vetches, alfalfa and other leguminous crops will especially benefit from its application. But slags vary in content, so check the analysis before using. Avoid slags with low or nonexistent amounts of nutrients and trace elements. Don't use slags containing excessive amounts of sulfur.

Beet wastes: Residues from sugar beet processing are commonly used for livestock feed, though they will compost readily in heaps or as sheet compost. The nitrogen content averages 0.4 percent, potassium content varies from 0.7 to 4.1 percent, and phosphoric acid content ranges from 0.1 to 0.6 percent. Dried beet pulp is also available at many feed stores.

Blood: Dried blood is a slaughterhouse by-product. It is high in nitrogen, about 12 percent, but its phosphorus content varies from 1 to 5 percent. Blood meal is used, ironically, as an animal feed, though most garden shops carry it for use as a fertilizer. The cost is quite high per pound; the price is tied to the rising price of meat. Blood meal can be applied directly to the soil around plants, but it should be kept several inches away from the stems. Blood meal will burn. Dried blood may also be used in compost heaps. Sprinkle it over layers of moist organic matter. The high nitrogen content will stimulate decay organisms, especially if the material you're using is rich in carbon.

Bone meal: Another slaughterhouse by-product, the pulverized residue of bones is, along with rock phosphate, a major source of phosphorus for the farm and garden. Bone meal also contains a large percentage of nitrogen, though the content of both minerals depends on the age and type of bones processed. Raw bone meal usually contains 20 to 25 percent phosphoric acid and 2 to 4 percent nitrogen. Steamed bone meal, the more commonly available variety, has up to 30 percent phosphorus and 1 to 2 percent nitrogen. Steamed bone meal is finer than bone meal in the raw state, thus breaking down more rapidly in the soil or compost heap.

Bone black or charred bone is another type of bone residue, containing about 1.5 percent nitrogen, 30 percent phosphoric acid and many trace elements.

Bone meals are most effective when mixed with other organic matter and added to well-aerated soils. They will also exert an alkalizing effect because of their lime content, so match their use to your soil's pH characteristics. Use moderately in composting so as not to encourage the volatilization of nitrogen. (See the note on using lime in compost making, earlier.)

Bone meal is an excellent plant food providing both phosphorus and nitrogen, but it contains lime and therefore should be used only moderately in the compost pile

Buckwheat hulls: Buckwheat is a cereal crop grown mainly in northeastern U.S. and in Canada. Popular among organic farmers and gardeners as a green manure and bee forage crop, it will grow well on even marginal soils. Buckwheat hulls, left after processing of the grain, are lightweight and disk shaped. They make good additions to the compost heap if you can get them in quantity, though many gardeners prefer to use them as mulch. The hulls absorb water easily, stay in place once applied (a layer 1½ inches thick will suffice) and look like a crumbly loam.

Castor pomace: This would be available as a by-product from a factory producing castor oil. The pomace is the residue left after the castor beans have gone through the oil extraction process. Nitrogen content varies from 4 to 6.6 percent. Potassium and phosphoric acid run about 1 to 2 percent, with more variation in the phosphorus content.

Castor pomace makes an excellent compost activator if manure or other animal sources of nitrogen are unavailable. Wet the pomace into a slurry, and mix it well with absorbent organic matter.

Citrus wastes: Gardeners living near factories producing orange and grapefruit products should make use of this easily composted residue, though dried citrus pulp is also available in bulk from some feed stores. The nitrogen content of these materials varies according to the type of fruit and the density of the skin. The thicker the peel, the more nitrogen contained.

Orange skins contain about 3 percent phosphoric acid and 27 percent potash (surpassed only by banana skins with 50 percent potash). Lemons are higher in phosphorus but lower in potash than oranges. Grapefruits average 3.6 percent phosphoric acid, and their potassium content is near that of oranges.

You may also use whole waste fruits (culls) in the compost pile, although their nutrient content will be lower due to the high water content. Citrus wastes will break down faster if shredded (the bagged, dried pulp sold as animal feed comes in dime-size chips) and mixed with green matter and a source of nitrogen and bacteria like manure, lawn clippings or garden soil.

Unfortunately, citrus crops are routinely sprayed by commercial growers. If the spray program is moderate, the chemicals should break down in the soil and composting process without causing harm.

Cocoa bean shells: These residues from chocolate factories are available in bulk from garden supply houses, but because they make such an attractive mulch they rarely find their way into the compost heap. They are rich in nutrients, though, and benefit the soil however they're used. Cocoa shell dust has 1.5 percent phosphorus, about 1.7 percent potassium and 1 percent nitrogen—a high analysis of the latter considering the woody nature of cocoa.

If the shells themselves have been treated to extract the caffeine and theobromine, the residues will have about 2.7 percent nitrogen, 0.7 percent phosphoric acid and 2.6 percent of potassium. Untreated raw shells show a higher nutrient content. Pressed cocoa cake has also been offered as fertilizer. It's higher in nitrogen, has less potassium than shells and has a phosphorus content of nearly 0.9 percent. The nitrogen content of cake will vary according to its processing.

Cocoa bean hulls are a popular mulch for both edibles and ornamentals, but their nutrient content makes them a good compost ingredient, too

If you can locate a source of oil-free and theobromine-free cocoa wastes, you'll have a useful product for mulching acidic soils. The extraction process uses lime, so the shells will help raise the pH while adding moisture-retentive organic matter. Cocoa shells are also weed-free and odorless.

To use as mulch, spread the shells in a layer 1 inch deep. They are light brown, look nice around shrubs, evergreens and flower beds and offer excellent drought-proofing and insulative properties. Shells used in compost piles should be shredded or pulverized for rapid decay.

Coffee wastes: Earthworms seem to have a particular affinity for coffee grounds, so be sure to use these leftovers on the compost pile or as a mulch. The grounds are acidic and can be used by themselves around blueberries, evergreens and other acid-loving plants. Mix the grounds with a little ground limestone for plants needing alkaline or neutral soil.

The nutrient content of coffee residues varies according to the type of residue. Grounds have up to 2 percent

Coffee grounds are good to use in composting, but their acidity will need to be neutralized

nitrogen, 0.33 percent phosphoric acid and varying amounts of potassium. Drip coffee grounds contain more nutrients than boiled grounds, though the potassium content is still below 1 percent. Other substances found include sugars, carbohydrates, some vitamins, trace elements and caffeine.

Coffee processing plants sell coffee chaff, a dark material containing over 2 percent nitrogen and potassium. Chaff is useful either as a mulch or in compost.

Apply your coffee grounds immediately, or mix them with other organic matter. They hold moisture extremely well. Left standing, they will quickly sour, inviting acetobacters (vinegar-producing microbes) and fruit flies.

Many gardeners are enthusiastic about using coffee grounds, claiming that their application has a dramatic effect on the growth and health of various plants.

Corn cobs: These residues used to be available in large amounts from mills, but modern combines now shred the stalks and expel the cobs right back into the field. Cobs contain two-thirds of the nutrients found in the corn kernel, but they must be shredded before composting or their decay will take years. Let the cobs age in open piles for several months, then grind them with a shredder or lawn mower.

Cobs have superior moisture retention and make effective mulches when spread 3 to 4 inches deep. Shredded cobs may also be used as a seed-starting medium. In long-standing, no-turn piles, unshredded cobs mixed with leaves and other dense materials will provide aeration and discourage caking and matting.

Cottonseed meal: With a nitrogen content of 7 percent, this by-product of the cotton industry will help create hot compost where gardeners don't have access to manure. It may also be used directly as a sidedressing, supplying 1.5 percent potash and 2 to 3 percent phosphoric acid.

Cottonseed meal is derived from dehulled cottonseed with the oil and lint removed. The resultant cake is high in protein and used extensively as stock feed. Only a fraction is actually marketed as fertilizer.

The material is acidic and best used around plants and crops preferring a low pH. To use cottonseed meal as a compost activator, sprinkle it over moist layers of materials with a low nitrogen content.

Dolomite: This is a mineral deposit which, when quarried and pulverized, is sold as a liming agent. Dolomitic limestone is preferred by many gardeners over calcic limestone because it has a higher magnesium content. Pure dolomitic lime would contain almost 46 percent magnesium carbonate and 54 percent calcium carbonate. (See the note on using lime in the compost pile.)

Earthworms: Cool, long-standing compost heaps that are not turned frequently will benefit from the addition of earthworms. Many of the creatures will work their way into the pile from below, breeding and increasing in number rapidly if the food supply and temperature are adequate. Worms may also be added to the heap, but do this only if you've built a cool pile (one that won't heat above 110°F) or if you want worms in a heap after the high heat stage has passed. Dig worms right from a vacant part of your property (or nearby woods or fields) rather than buying the special red worms or wrigglers. The latter are specialized worms that must live in manure or raw organic matter. They will not survive long in garden soil, so you'd have to remove or sacrifice them when you apply the finished compost. (See the note on worms in the previous chapter How Compost Affects Soil.)

Felt wastes: Check hat factories for discarded hair, wool and felt. These materials may contain up to 14 percent nitrogen and will aid in making rapid, high heat compost. Such wastes are quite dry, however, and will decompose slowly or pack down unless they are thoroughly moistened and mixed with bacteria-rich ingredients like manure or green matter.

Fish scraps: Gardeners near oceans or fish processing plants can usually truck home loads of this smelly stuff. It is well supplied with nitrogen and phosphorus (7 percent or above for each nutrient) and also contains valuable trace elements like iodine. But, like all fresh residues, fish scraps easily turn anaerobic and are highly attractive to rodents, flies and other scavengers.

Fish scraps must be handled carefully in the garden, either buried (covered with at least 4 to 6 inches of soil) or composted in properly built heaps enclosed by sturdy bins or pens. Mix with absorbent plant matter (sawdust, hay or dead leaves) to increase aeration and discourage packing down.

Composting fish scraps in a pit is somewhat easier (once you've dug the pit, of course). Mix them with organic matter or soil and cover with enough dirt to discourage flies. The pit must also be enclosed by a sturdy fence or wall and topped with a scavenger-proof frame or lid.

Kitchen garbage is one of our most overlooked resources that should be recycled by home gardeners and on a larger scale, too

Garbage: Americans routinely throw away mountains of valuable food scraps, setting them out on the curb or grinding them up in disposals and flushing them into overworked municipal sewage systems. Yet kitchen scraps are truly a neglected resource, containing 1 to 3 percent nitrogen along with calcium, phosphorus, potassium and trace minerals. The material is free, available in quantity every day and relatively easy to handle.

Kitchen scraps may be dug directly into the garden (see the section Trenching or Compostholing in the chapter How to Make Compost, found earlier in this book). Alternatively, they may be composted in heaps or pits. Mix well with absorbent matter like dead leaves or hay to offset the wetness. Use a predator-proof enclosure, and be sure to keep all scraps well into the pile's core, covering them thoroughly with dirt or additional materials to discourage flies. (This is only necessary at the beginning stages of composting. A high heat pile is capable of almost totally digesting most kitchen scraps within 48 hours.)

Chop or shred all large pieces of matter (potatoes, grapefruit rinds, eggshells, etc.) to hasten decomposition. Do not use meat scraps, fat or bones in compost piles, for these materials take too long to fully break down.

Gin trash: This isn't the residue from a saloon: it's a by-product of the cotton industry. Once burned and discarded, these leaf and stem wastes are now being composted and returned to the soil. But while cotton wastes do contain many valuable nutrients and fibrous organic matter, their effect on soil health may not be beneficial. Arsenic is routinely used in California, Texas and Oklahoma as a defoliant and desiccant. Significant residues of this carcinogen are left in the gin trash. Normal arsenic levels in the soil run about 5 parts per million, but gin wastes may contain 40 times that amount.

Cottonseed meal, however, is safe to use. Produced in a completely different manner, the meal contains arsenic only in the 0.05 parts per million range. This amount is probably naturally occurring, because arsenic used on the cotton crops does not get into the seeds. (See Cottonseed meal, earlier in this chapter.)

Granite dust: This is a natural source of potash that is superior to the chemically treated potash sold as commercial fertilizer. Granite dust or granite meal has a potassium content of between 3 and 5 percent, contains trace elements, is inexpensive and will leave no harmful chemical residues. Unlike chemically treated sources of potash, granite dust is slow acting, releasing its nutrients over a period of years. It may be used in the compost pile or added to soil or sheet compost. Use it liberally directly on the soil, applying 10 pounds to 100 square feet when spreading. Choose a windless day for application, and wear a dust mask.

Grape wastes: Wineries produce these residues of skins, seeds and stalks by the ton during the pressing season. Vineyards also accumulate large amounts of grapevine pieces after annual pruning. While the nutrient content of grape wastes isn't that high, the sheer bulk of organic materials involved benefits the soil by promoting aeration and microbial activity.

The residues of pressing will be wet and mushy and should be mixed with absorbent plant matter. Additional nitrogen in the form of manure or high-protein green matter may also be necessary if you desire rapid, hot compost. The prunings are tough and must be chopped into pieces 3 to 6 inches long if they are to break down in a season.

Grass clippings: This is one compostable—a true "green manure"—that most suburbanites and some city dwellers can produce in abundance. Even if you don't have your own lawn, your fellow citizens do; they'll leave bags of clippings conveniently lined up along the curbsides for your harvesting every garbage collection day.

Freshly gathered green clippings are exceedingly rich in nitrogen and will heat up on their own if pulled into a pile. But, because of their high water content, they will also pack down and become slimy. Always mix grass clippings with dead leaves or other dry matter. Grass clippings and leaves can be turned into finished compost in two weeks if the heap is chopped and turned every three days. (See the section titled Fast Composting in the chapter How to Make Compost, found earlier in this book, for rapid, hot composting techniques.) You can also profitably mix two-thirds grass clippings with one-third manure and bedding for a relatively fast compost, even if the pile is left unturned.

Never throw away grass clippings; use them as mulch or use them for compost, but by all means use them

Clippings also make an excellent mulch in the vegetable or flower garden or around shrubs and trees. As a mulch, clippings look neat and stay in place, and only a light layer (3 to 4 inches) is needed to choke out weeds and seal in moisture. Clippings can also be dug directly into the soil. The material will cause a temporary nitrogen deficiency when green, but this will be short-lived because the clippings are fine enough to break down rapidly. Also, because they contain an abundance of nitrogen, decay bacteria can feed on them without pulling much of that nutrient from the soil itself.

There is one environmental caution about grass clippings, however. Many homeowners use various "weed and feed" preparations or any of a half-dozen herbicides in striving for an immaculate lawn. The most troublesome of these chemicals is 2,4–D, a preemergent weed killer that has caused birth defects in lab animals and may be carcinogenic.

Although this systemic rapid-action plant hormone attacks broadleaf plants like dandelions, literally causing them to grow themselves to death in hours, 2,4–D doesn't affect grasses. The narrow-bladed leaves <u>do</u> absorb traces of the hormone but not enough to harm them. Much more 2,4–D remains as a residue in broadleaf plants, though even this should theoretically be broken down by soil microbes in a week. But beware of grass clippings that may have spray adhering to them from a fresh application.

Ask your neighbors or whoever you gather clippings from what they use on their lawns. (If several mowings and some rains have occurred since the last application of herbicide, the clippings should be clear of 2,4–D residue.) Use your own clippings if you have them, and look around for natural lawns showing a healthy crop of dandelions—a sign that the landowner wisely avoided using herbicides.

Greensand: This is an undersea mineral deposit containing traces of most (if not all) the naturally occurring elements found in seawater. Also known as glauconite greensand or greensand marl, it is an iron-potassium silicate that has been used as a valuable soil-builder for over a century.

Greensand is an excellent source of potassium; its potassium content actually available to plants is 6 to 7 percent. Good glauconite deposits also contain 50 percent silica, 18 to 23 percent iron oxides, 3 to 7.5 percent magnesia, small amounts of lime and phosphoric acid and traces of more than 30 other elements useful to higher plant life.

Greensand is available from organically minded garden shops and from mail-order suppliers of seeds and tools.

Hair: Between 6 and 7 pounds of hair contain as much nitrogen as 100 to 200 pounds of manure. Like feathers, hair will decompose rapidly in a compost pile but only if well moistened and thoroughly mixed with an aerating material. Hair tends to pack down and shed water, so chopping or turning the pile regularly will hasten decay. Most barbershops or beauty salons will be happy to supply you with bags of hair (though they may think your request is strange unless you explain).

Hoof and Horn meal: Like most slaughterhouse by-products, these are high in nitrogen. A 100-pound sack contains 10 to 16 pounds of actual nitrogen, as much as a ton of manure. The phosphoric acid content runs about 2 percent.

Hoof and horn meal comes in several grades. Finely ground horn dust is best for general compost, soil amending and potting soil as it dissolves rapidly. Granular meal is more difficult to handle. It will break down slowly and attract flies unless kept moist and covered with additional organic matter or soil.

Hops: This is a viny plant grown and used for making beer. (Hops impart the characteristic bitter flavor.) Spent hops, the wastes left after the brewing process, are an excellent garden fertilizer, containing (when dry) 2.5 to 3.5 percent nitrogen and 1 percent phosphoric acid. They do have a strong odor when wet and fresh, but this dissipates rapidly.

Wet hops may be spread directly on the garden in fall or spring just as you would apply manure. Turn the matter under, mixing with the top 4 to 6 inches of soil. Wet hops heat up rapidly, so keep them several inches away from plant stems to avoid burning. This tendency to heat up is, of course, desirable in making compost. Be sure to balance the sogginess of spent hops with absorbent matter.

Spent hops make a good mulch when dry. They resist blowing away and will not easily ignite if a lighted match or cigarette is tossed onto a pile. A 6-inch layer of dry, spent hops will break down slowly, staying put for three years or more.

Another brewery waste to inquire about is the grain left over from the mashing process. When wet, this material contains almost 1 percent nitrogen and decays rapidly.

Leather dust: Available from garden shops and from leather processors, this is a high-nitrogen material containing from 5.5 to 12 percent of the nutrient. Phosphorus is also present in considerable amounts. Use as a soil amendment, as a sidedressing around plants or as a dusting over successive layers in the compost heap.

Leaves: Here's another valuable compostable and mulch material abundantly available to most gardeners. Because trees have extensive root systems, they draw nutrients up from deep within the subsoil. Much of this mineral bounty is passed into the leaves, making them a superior garden resource. Pound for pound, most tree leaves contain twice the mineral content of manure. The considerable fiber content of leaves also aids in improving the aeration and crumb structure of most soils.

Many people shy away from using leaves in compost because they've had trouble with them packing down and resisting decay. Leaves don't contain much nitrogen, so a pile of them all alone may take years to decay fully. But most leaves can be converted to a fine textured humus in several weeks (or, at most, a few months) if some general guides are followed:

A pound of tree leaves usually contains twice as many minerals as a pound of manure

1. Shred the leaves with a power lawn mower or shredder to increase their surface area. You can also chop the leaves once they're mixed with other organic matter and piled in a heap. Instead of turning the mass with a pitchfork, slice away with a 10-pound mattock or heavy grubbing hoe. The moist leaves will fragment, mix thoroughly with the nitrogenous matter and decay quickly.

2. Additional nitrogen must be supplied to leaves to offset their high carbon content. Mix 5 parts leaves to 1 part manure (by weight, not volume). Or use a 50-50 mix of fresh grass clippings and leaves (by volume, not weight). If you don't have any manure or grass clippings, use a nitrogen supplement such as soybean or cottonseed meal, dried blood, bone meal or leather dust. Several cups of these ingredients should be sprinkled over each wheelbarrow of leaves. Be sure the leaves are thoroughly moistened, or no heat will develop, regardless of how much dry nitrogen you add.

Leaves can also be turned into black, fine leaf mold by simply piling them up, wetting them thoroughly and enclosing them for several years out in the open. Leaf mold doesn't contain the nutrients found in composted leaves, but it's an excellent soil-builder when used liberally as well as an attractive mulch. The material is acidic, though, and you may wish to dust it with lime if your soil already has a low pH.

Limestone: While not a fertilizer, lime is a necessity in gardens with acid soil (see the chart How Much Lime to Add in the chapter How Compost Affects Soil, found earlier in this book, for general application rates). While supplying calcium (and magnesium if dolomitic lime is used), lime's prime importance is its role as an alkalizer and its physical effect on the soil. Lime breaks up sticky clay particles and binds loose sand grains, creating better drainage in the former and water retention in the latter. But lime is best applied directly to the soil instead of being used in the compost pile (see A Note on Using Lime in the Compost Pile, earlier in this chapter).

Manure: Animal wastes, both solid and liquid, are critically important ingredients in the composting and soil-building processes. You can make an active compost pile and valuable humus without manure, but its addition greatly speeds up the decay process while contributing many nutrients to soil and plant life. As much as one-third of dung's mass is bacteria, so even a small amount added to a working compost heap will activate the rapid decomposition of the other organic materials.

Much of manure's value to the soil depends on how it is handled. Half the fertilizer value of manure is lost within four days when the material is merely spread on the ground in a thin layer. Manure piled in heaps and exposed to rain rapidly loses nutrients by leaching.

For best results, begin composting manure and bedding as soon as you can after removing them from the barn. Or spread and dig it under on the same day. If rapid use isn't feasible, then keep manure covered with a tarp or plastic sheeting.

Each type of manure has its own characteristics:

● Chicken: A hot manure richest in N–P–K. It will burn plants if allowed to come in direct contact. Poultry litter is usually well mixed with bedding (leaves, straw, etc.) so it's easy to moisten the mass and begin a very hot pile. Add carboniferous matter if necessary, or you'll lose considerable nitrogen as ammonia.

● Horse: Another hot manure, though easier to handle than poultry litter. Horse manure contains more nitrogen than cow or pig dung and will heat up rapidly. For best results, mix it with plenty of carboniferous material and adequate moisture.

● Pig: Concentrated but relatively lower in nitrogen, pig wastes ferment slowly. Mix with other types of manure and a large volume of green or dry plant matter.

● Sheep and Goat: Sheep produce a high-nitrogen manure, goats less so. But both manures are pelleted and can be mixed easily with plant wastes.

● Cow: Hard to handle unless mixed with ample bedding, fresh cow manure is wet, heavy and relatively low in nitrogen. Mix with other types of manure and green plant matter as it ferments slowly.

● Rabbit: Higher in nitrogen than some poultry manure, rabbit "pellets" also contain a large percentage of phosphoric acid. Rabbit dung is a hot manure and will quickly activate a pile of mixed plant wastes. Like sheep and goat droppings, rabbit manure is relatively dry and easy to handle.

● Human urine: Collecting your own and your family's urine may strike you as bizarre, but the practice makes good sense. Urban gardeners in particular have a difficult time securing adequate amounts of manure for their gardens and compost, and all gardeners have a need for supplemental nitrogen. Human urine is always available and free, and it is high in soluble nitrogen. (But see the caution earlier in this chapter, in the section What Not to Use in a Compost Pile, about using solid human waste.)

Cow manure is the most widely used animal manure, but other types are higher in nutrients

According to expert gardeners Bill and Helga Olkowski of Berkeley, California, who recommend using urine in city compost piles and vegetable plots, you can supply the equivalent of 200 pounds of nitrogen per acre to your garden with urine. Apply 2 quarts of urine for every 27 square feet (3 by 9 feet) every two weeks. Dilute the urine with five parts of water if possible. All urine is alkaline, containing salt and urea, which may be retained in the soil, particularly if your area gets little rain and you use urine frequently. Leach this excess salt away by adding about a quarter pound of lime to each 25 square feet of garden area. Do this annually.

Adding urine to your compost pile is easier. Simply sprinkle it on with a watering can. It won't draw flies or produce odors.

The only problem in using human urine, however, is

neighborhood disapproval and, perhaps, outrage. After all, "normal" behavior is to use 5 gallons of water to flush away half a cup of urine. So be discreet—at least until society recognizes you as a pioneer.

Molasses residues: The wastes from sugar refining are obviously rich in carbohydrates, but they also contain some mineral nutrients. Naturally occurring yeasts in the compost will ferment these sugars rapidly. Dry molasses is also available from feed stores.

Olive wastes: Olive pits contain phosphorus, nitrogen and some lignin (a woody substance related to cellulose). But the pits must be ground or chopped before composting, or they'll take years to decay. Pulpy olive wastes vary in nutrient density. One analysis showed the pomace (what's left after oil extraction) having 1.15 percent nitrogen, 0.78 percent phosphoric acid and 1.26 percent potassium. The pulp is oily and should be well mixed with other organic matter.

Peat moss: This naturally occurring fibrous material is the centuries-old, partially decayed residue of plants. Widely sold as a soil conditioner, mulch and plant propagation medium, peat's major advantages are its water retention (it is capable of absorbing 15 times its weight in water) and fibrous bulk. Dry peat will help loosen heavy soils, bind light ones, hold nutrients in place and increase aeration. But while its physical effects on soil are valuable, peat isn't a substitute for compost. Expensive, relatively low in nutrients and acidic, peat is best used as a seed flat and rooting medium or as a mulch or soil amendment for acid-loving plants.

Pea wastes: Feeding pea shells and vines to livestock and getting it back as manure is an excellent recycling method. Otherwise, pea wastes can be rapidly composted since they are rich in nitrogen when green. Dry vines should be shredded or chopped before or during composting to hasten decay. Diseased vines should be burned and the ashes returned to the soil. (Pea ash contains almost 3 percent phosphoric acid and 27 percent potassium.)

Pet litter: Dog droppings from healthy pets are safe to use in compost piles in limited amounts. While rich in nutrients, dog manure is more difficult and less pleasant to handle than the mixed bedding and manure of cows and horses. Some dog owners use a special compost pile or pit to receive dog wastes.

Avoid cat droppings totally, especially if you or someone in the household is pregnant or if you have small children. Cat manure may contain Toxoplasma gondii, a one-celled organism that when transmitted to a pregnant woman may infect her unborn child, causing brain and eye disease. Cat droppings may also contain Toxocara cati, a roundworm that may cause similar problems in children. Keep the contents of the litter box away from children and the compost pile.

Wastewater from aquariums is safe to use on house plants and in the garden.

Wastes from pet cats and birds should not be used in the compost pile

Phosphate rock: This is a mainstay in organic gardens and farms because of its value as a soil and compost pile amendment. While its chemical composition varies according to the source, phosphate rock generally contains 65 percent calcium phosphate or bone phosphate of lime. A diversity of other compounds and trace elements important to plant development is also present.

Phosphate rock is a naturally occurring mineral, however; don't confuse it with superphosphate. The latter has been treated with sulfuric acid to increase its solubility. But many trace elements are lost due to this processing, and the increase in the availability of sulfur stimulates the presence of sulfur-reducing bacteria in the soil. These organisms attack sulfur and also ingest a fungus that normally breaks down cellulose in the soil. Besides encouraging this microbial imbalance, superphosphate can also leave harmful salts in the soil.

Phosphate rock creates no such problems. It's slow acting, which makes nutrients available to plants for many years after a single application. Applied alone to vegetable or flower gardens, 1 pound to every 10 square feet of growing area will suffice for three to five years. It may also be sprinkled lightly over succeeding layers in a compost heap to add nutrients to the finished product.

Pine needles: These are acidic and tough to compost. Cutin, a waxy substance coating the exterior of the needles, makes them decay slowly. Shredding speeds the process. Use pine needles liberally in composting only if you want to make an acidic humus or lower the pH of an alkaline soil.

Potash rock: Like other naturally occurring rock fertilizers, potash rock can be used on soils with no danger of overdose. This inexpensive rock, which contains a large amount of potassium, may be used alone on most soils or in compost piles. The usual recommendation for gardens is 2 ⅓ pounds per 100 square feet. Potash rock is generally available throughout the country.

Potato wastes: Potato peels are common components of kitchen scraps. They provide a valuable source of nitrogen (about 0.6 percent as ash) and trace elements for the compost pile. Rotted whole potatoes, chopped or shredded, would also be a worthwhile compostable. The tubers contain about 2.5 percent potash, plus other minerals. Use the potato vines, too; they can either be composted or dug back into the soil. The vines, when dry, contain approximately 1.6 percent potash, 4 percent calcium and 1.1 percent magnesium, plus sulfur and other minerals.

Rice hulls: Gardeners in the Texas-Louisiana Gulf Coast area may be able to get this useful soil conditioner and compostable from local rice mills. The hulls break down rapidly, contain much potassium and make an excellent mulch that won't blow away. Some mills burn the hulls, but even the ash is valuable because the potassium is more concentrated.

Sawdust: Many gardeners fear this widely available and inexpensive (or free) material because they mistakenly think it will acidify their soil or create a nitrogen deficiency. Raw sawdust ties up soil nitrogen as it decays, just as any other raw organic matter does, but the nitrogen loss is temporary. Raw sawdust can be used as a mulch, however, with no nitrogen loss whatever. A layer 2 inches thick is attractive, conserves moisture, smothers weeds and eventually adds to the soil's humus content.

Don't dig raw sawdust into the soil until the end of the growing season, when it can decay without interfering with plant development.

Extensive tests conducted by the Connecticut Experimental Station (1949 to 1954) demonstrated that the regular application of sawdust and wood chips will not make acid soils more acid. But its extensive use on the extremely alkaline soils found in the western United States might help buffer the pH toward neutral.

Sawdust is very low in nitrogen, so composting it rapidly will require lots of nitrogenous matter like manure or protein-rich green matter. The easiest way to accomplish this, when practical, is to use sawdust as livestock bedding. Cleaning the barn will then yield a readily compostable mix of sawdust, urine and manure. (See also Wood chips, found later in this section.)

Seaweed: Coastal gardeners can gather different types of seaweed by wandering the shoreline. Look for kelp (laminaria), bladder wrack (also called fucus), sea lettuce (ulva) and other varieties. Gardeners elsewhere can buy dried, granulated seaweed or liquid concentrate. All these seaweed variants are rich in many types of trace elements and are a boon to plants, soil health and the compost pile.

Compared to barnyard manure, seaweed in general has a similar organic content. The proportions, however, vary: seaweed has more potassium than manure but has less nitrogen and phosphorus.

Use wet, fresh seaweed quickly, because it deteriorates rapidly when piled haphazardly. Dig the seaweed under, or mix it with nitrogenous and absorbent materials for rapid composting. Bacteria feast on the alginic acid found in the leaves, which makes seaweed an excellent compost pile activator.

Seaweed is rich in trace minerals and makes an excellent plant food and compost ingredient

If you only have a small amount of seaweed, chop it and soak it overnight in a gallon of hot water (160° to 180°F). Sprinkle this mixture over successive layers of the compost pile. The liquid can also be used as a spray for plants (it has some insect- and fungus-repellent properties), as a liquid fertilizer and as a soaking water for seeds. Liquid seaweed made from concentrate or granular seaweed may be used the same way. Dry seaweed powder may be used as a sidedressing.

Sewage sludge: While rich in nutrients and an excellent way to recycle human wastes, sewage sludge must be considered a questionable or dangerous material for use in the garden or compost pile. Sludge is the solid residue left after organic wastes and wastewater have been chemically, bacterially or physically processed. Depending on how it was processed, sludge may contain up to 6 percent nitrogen.

Until recently, most sewage sludge was incinerated, buried in landfills or dumped offshore. Now there's an increasing interest in using this potentially valuable material as a soil conditioner. This would be ideal if the residue was composed solely of the remains of human waste, but that isn't the case.

In most instances, city sewage is an unregulated mixture of industrial and residential waste. The resultant sludge is often contaminated with toxic amounts of heavy metals; cadmium is the most troublesome. While other heavy metals such as copper, zinc and nickel can be dangerous to humans, a high concentration of them in soil would be obvious. Plants would turn yellow, wither and die.

Not so with cadmium. Plants readily absorb large amounts of this substance without showing signs of toxicity. The health of people or livestock who eat the contaminated plants is in danger, because cadmium has been linked to cancer and kidney damage.

There are many indirect ways cadmium can get into your garden soil. Nearby auto traffic can deposit it, as can polluted air or water from industry. However, applying contaminated sludge to your land or compost heap can boost cadmium levels into the toxic range overnight, thereby causing permanent damage to your soil.

So don't use sludge without first asking a lot of questions and getting detailed answers. Has your city's sludge been tested and analyzed? Does your community support industry whose wastes are discharged into the municipal sewage system?

Electronics firms, zinc smelters, photoengravers and manufacturers of light bulbs, pigments, batteries and PVC may all contribute to contaminated sludge. Unless you're absolutely sure of the chemical content of your community's sludge, don't apply it near or on food crops or anywhere that runoff might contaminate a garden, orchard or well.

Soil: While not a necessity, soil is a valuable component in compost making. The thin (⅛-inch) layer called for in Indore heaps contains billions of soil organisms that consume plant, animal and mineral matter, converting it to humus. Soil also contains minerals and organic matter so it acts like an activator when added to compostables.

Thin layers of dirt in the compost heap work to absorb unstable substances produced by fermentation, thereby slowing their loss to the atmosphere. And when the pile is built, a topping of several inches of topsoil will stop heat and water from leaving the pile. Don't add too much soil, however, or the finished compost will be quite heavy to handle.

Other than your own property, sources for soil include nearby woods, fields, building excavations and mud from streams and ponds free of industrial or agricultural pollution. Don't use pond or stream mud directly in your soil, because it will have the same effect on nitrogen as adding raw manure. Mud is also easier to handle if you dry it before composting by mixing it with layers of absorbent plant wastes.

Spanish moss: This plant is not a true moss but a seed plant of the pineapple family that is used by mattress, furniture and upholstery manufacturers. Gardeners in the Deep South should visit local moss gins (Louisiana has hundreds), where the residues of cleaned moss are piled up like sawdust. Use it in the compost pile or as a mulch. A thin layer forms an impenetrable barrier against weeds.

Straw: While low in nutrients and high in carbon, straw is useful in the compost heap or as mulch because it helps balance the excess moisture of extremely wet materials like fresh manure. It's also inexpensive and plentiful. Straw must be thoroughly mixed with moist, high-nitrogen materials or its decomposition will take several seasons. Chop or shred straw for faster results. Straw used as livestock bedding is ideal for hot composting.

Straw, especially straw that's been used in stables, is a good addition to the compost pile — it is cheap and abundant

Sugar wastes: The most plentiful sugar processing residue is burned bone or bone charcoal, which is used as a filtration medium. Called bone black when saturated with sugar residues, this substance contains 2 percent nitrogen, more than 30 percent phosphorus and a variable potassium content. Raw sugar residues have over 1 percent nitrogen and over 8 percent phosphoric acid.

Tanbark: Tanbark is plant waste that remains following the tanning of leather. Its residues are shredded, heaped and inoculated with decay-promoting bacteria. Thus composted, tanbark is sold in bulk as mulching material. Analysis shows nitrogen at 1.7 percent, phosphorus at 0.9 percent and potassium at 0.2 percent; various trace minerals are also present. Like peat, tanbark makes an excellent mulch but is too expensive to use extensively in compost making.

Tankage: Although this residue of slaughterhouses and butcher shops is abundant in nutrients, it's hard to use in the home garden. Meat and fat don't break down easily, and unless they are handled with care, they'll attract flies, rodents and neighborhood complaints about the stench. The nitrogen content of tankage runs between 5 and 12.5 percent, and its phosphorus content is about 2 percent. The latter may be much higher, depending on the amount of bone present in the refuse.

Tea grounds: You'll have to save a lot of those little bags to make heavy use of this residue, but it might be worth it. Tea leaves have a surprisingly high nitrogen content of 4.15 percent. However, both their phosphorus and potash content is low, under 1 percent for each substance.

Tobacco: Tobacco wastes can be profitably composted, used as mulch or incorporated into the soil as sheet compost. An assay of the stems, leaves and dust shows that 100 pounds of tobacco residue contains 2.5 to 3.7 pounds of nitrogen, almost 1 pound of phosphorus and an especially high percentage of potassium, 4.5 to 7 pounds.

If you live in tobacco-growing country and can obtain these wastes from farmers or processors (who may sell tobacco residues by the bale), use it as you would manure. Don't apply near tobacco, tomatoes or other members of the tobacco or potato family because they are all subject to similar viral diseases, particularly tobacco mosaic.

And don't use tobacco wastes alone as a mulch. Mix them with other organic matter, since the nicotine in concentrated amounts will leach out and subsequently kill soil organisms, earthworms and some beneficial insects.

Residues from tobacco plants (not cigarettes) can be a useful compost ingredient when handled carefully

Water hyacinth: This is an aquatic pest in many southern streams, where it grows in lush profusion. A check with your local environmental, fisheries, agriculture or water agency may net you heaps of this green matter. Shred and chop it up for rapid decomposition, and mix it with a bacterial activator like soil or manure.

Weeds: "A weed," said Emerson, "is a plant for which we have yet to find a use." But gardeners can use almost all weeds to enrich their soil. Weeds can be allowed to grow, then later can be mowed, raked and used in the compost pile or as sheet compost. Chopped weeds can also be used as a mulch so long as they are cut before the seed heads have appeared. (Weed seeds will be destroyed when the hot compost pile attains temperatures of 140° to 160°F.) Various weeds are deeply rooted and bring ample minerals up into their leaves and stems.

Wood ashes: Although they are most valuable for their potassium content, wood ashes can also be used as a lime substitute to neutralize acid soil. Potassium percentages vary according to the type of wood burned. Hardwood residues contain from 1 to 10 percent potash, plus 1.5 percent phosphorus.

Ashes can also be used as a sidedressing around plants that do poorly in acid soil (beets, lettuce and members of the cabbage family, for example) for its nutrient content, and its insect- and slug-repelling qualities. Don't overuse wood ashes, though; a thin layer will suffice. Also keep ashes away from the roots of tender seedlings and germinating seeds.

Wood ashes may be used in the compost heap, but their effect will be similar to that of lime. (See a Note on

Using Lime in the Compost Pile, found earlier in this chapter.) Keep ashes stored under cover until use. Rain will quickly wash out the potash.

Wood chips: Mulching with wood chips is not only attractive but also effective. In addition, they can be worked into heavy soil to improve aeration, though they will tie up nitrogen temporarily while decaying. Till under in the fall or ahead of a green manure crop to minimize nitrogen tie-up.

Wood chips may also be used as livestock bedding and as a compost ingredient, especially where dense, wet materials need to be aerated. Because wood chips contain more bark, they tend to be somewhat richer in nutrients than sawdust (see Sawdust, found earlier in this section). Chips can be obtained from tree-care firms, highway and power line maintenance crews and sawmills.

Wool wastes: Also called "shoddy," these wastes are often available from textile mills and in smaller amounts from cottage industry weavers. Like hair, wool will decompose rapidly only when moist and well mixed with other materials to prevent it from packing down. Wool wastes generally contain 3.5 to 6 percent nitrogen, 2 to 4 percent phosphorus and 1 to 3.5 percent potash.

BIBLIOGRAPHY

The following books are recommended to gardeners who want further information on composting, soil management and good gardening practices.

Doscher, Paul; Fisher, Timothy; and Kolb, Kathleen. Intensive Gardening Year Round. Brattleboro, Vt.: Stephen Greene Press, 1980.
    For beginners, this book contains one of the best basic explanations of soil science. It also provides advice for beating the frosts.

Editors of Organic Gardening magazine. Getting the Most from Your Garden. Emmaus, Pa.: Rodale Press, 1980.
    A thorough guide to intensive gardening.

Minnich, Jerry. The Earthworm Book. Emmaus, Pa.: Rodale Press, 1977.
    More information on the original composters.

Minnich, Jerry; Hunt, Marjorie; and the editors of Organic Gardening magazine. The Rodale Guide to Composting. Emmaus, Pa.: Rodale Press, 1979.
    This is the most comprehensive book on the subject.

Seymour, John. The Self-Sufficient Gardener. Garden City, N.Y.: Doubleday & Co., 1979.
    A beautifully illustrated guide to intensive gardening of vegetables and fruits, written by a witty and experienced homesteader.

INDEX

A

Acid soil, measuring pH and, **94–98**
Aerobic compost piles, **6–7**
Air, composting and, **6**
Alfalfa, as compost material, **107**
Alkaline soil, measuring pH and, **94–98**
Anaerobic compost piles, **6**
Apartment, composting in, **31–34**
Apple pomace, as compost material, **107–8**

B

Bacteria, in compost pile
  mesophilic, **29**
  thermophilic, **29**
Bagasse, as compost material, **108**
Banana residues, as compost material, **108**
Basic slag, as compost material,
  application of, **108**
  minerals in, **108**
Beet wastes, as compost material, **109**
Bins, for composting, **37–38, 48–57**
  Lehigh, **50–51**
  modular slat, **51–52**
  New Zealand, **48–50**
  three-compartment block, **53–56**
  wood, **56–57**
Blood, dried, as compost material, **109**
Bone meal, as compost material, **109**
Bowing of compost frame, combating
  of, **50**

C

Cage pen, composting in, **47–48**
Carboniferous matter, composting
  and, **10**
Carbon/nitrogen (C/N) ratios
  compost pile and, **8–10**
  of organic materials, **9**

Castor pomace, as compost material, **110**
Cation exchange, process of, **89–92**
  measuring soil fertility and, **91**
Chicken manure, as compost material, **120**
Citrus waste, as compost material, **110–11**
Clay soil, **84–85**
  effect of humus on, **86**
Cocoa bean shells, as compost material,
  111
Coffee grounds, as compost material,
  111–12
  application of, **112**
  earthworms and, **111**
Compost
  application of, **70–82**
    in flower garden, **78–79**
    for house plants, **80–82**
    side-dressing, **73**
    for trees and shrubs, **79–80**
    in vegetable garden, **72–77**
  balancing pH and, **94–96**
  effect on soil, **83–85**
  materials for, **107–30**
Compost frames
  benefits of, **37**
  bins as, **37–38, 48–57**
  bowing, combating of, **50**
  hay bales as, **60**
  pens as, **38–48**
  plastic bag as, **62–63**
Compostholing method, **18–19**
Composting, **3–4**
  advantages of, **4**
  in apartments, **31–34**
  benefits of, **30–31**
  bins for, **37–38, 48–57**
  carboniferous matter and, **10**
  extending growing season and, **87**
  fast method, **6–7, 25–27**
  Indore method of, **7, 11–16**
  nitrogen for, **8–10**

pens for, **38–48**
various methods of, **11–34**
Compost materials
sources for, **100–104**
storage of, **68–69**
types of, **107–30**
which to avoid, **106–7**
Compost pile
aerobic, **6–7**
anaerobic, **6**
balancing moisture of, **7**
feeding air to, **6–7**
measuring temperature of, **28**
storing materials for, **68–69**
Compost pit, **57–60**
scavenger-proofing of, **58**
Compost tea
making barrel for, **64–68**
for watering garden, **63**
Compost water, use of, **74**
Corn cob, as compost material, **112**
Cottonseed meal, as compost
material, **112–13**
Cow manure, as compost material, **121**

D
Dolomite, as compost material, **113**

E
Earthworms
coffee grounds and, **111**
as compost ingredient, **113**
enrichment of soil and, **98–99**
permanent mulch and, **23**
pit composting and, **19, 38**

F
Farm, as source of compost material,
101–2
Feedlot, as source of compost material,
101
Felt waste, as compost material, **113**
Fertilizer, synthetic, **93**
effect on soil and, **89**
Fish scraps, as compost material, **113–14**

Flower garden
use of compost in, **78–79**
use of compost tea for, **78–79**
Freestanding piles, **36–37**

G
Garbage, household, as compost
material, **10, 114**
Gin trash, as compost material, **114–15**
Goat manure, as compost material, **121**
Granite dust, as compost material, **115**
Grape waste, as compost material, **115**
Grass clippings, as compost material,
116–17
Greensand, as compost material, **117**

H
Hair, as compost material, **117**
Hay bales, as compost frame, **60**
Hoof and horn meal, as compost
material, **117–18**
Hops, as compost material, **118**
Horse manure, as compost material,
120–21
Hot composting
benefits of, **30–31**
humic acids from, **30**
nitrogen and, **8**
House plants, compost for, **80–82**
Howard, Sir Albert
Indore compost method and, **11**
organic method and, **11**
Humic acids, hot composting and, **30**
Humus, **2–4**

I
Indore composting method, **7, 11–16**
advantages of, **16**
disadvantages of, **16**
Sir Albert Howard and, **11**

L
Leather dust, as compost material, **118**
Leaves, as compost material, **118–19**

Lehigh bin, composting in, **50–51**
Limestone
   adding to compost pile, **97, 105, 120**
   making potting soil and, **80**
Loam, **84–85**

M
Manure, as compost material, **120–22**
Mesophilic bacteria, **29**
Microbial life, needed in compost, **5–6**
Mills and factories, as source for
   compost material, **102**
Modular slat bin, composting in, **51–52**
Moisture, balancing of, and compost
   pile, **7**
Molasses residues, as compost material,
   122
Mulch
   applied to fruit trees, **80**
   compost as, **77**

N
New Zealand bin, compost in, **48–50**
Nitrogen, need for in compost, **8–10**

O
Olive wastes, as compost material, **122**
Orchard, as source of compost material,
   101–2
Organic matter, conversion to humus, **5**
Organic method, Sir Albert Howard on, **11**

P
Peat moss, as compost material, **122**
Pea wastes, as compost material, **122**
Pens, for composting, **38–48**
   cage, **47–48**
   knockdown, **43**
   portable, **40–42**
   snow fencing, **45**
   wire, **43–45**
   wood pallet, **46–47**
Permanent mulch, **21–25**
   drawbacks of, **24**
134

   earthworms for, **23**
   Ruth Stout on, **23–24**
Pet litter, as compost material, **123**
pH, level in soil
   adjusting of, **96–98**
   balancing with compost, **94–96**
   raising with limestone, **97–98**
Phosphate rock, as compost material, **123**
Pine needles, as compost material, **124**
Pit composting, **19-20, 57–60**
   disadvantages of, **38**
   earthworms for, **19, 38**
Plastic bag, composting in, **62–63**
Potash rock, as compost material, **124**
Potato wastes, as compost material, **124**
Potting soil, making of, and limestone, **80**

R
Rabbit pellets, as compost material, **121**
Rice hulls, as compost material, **124**
Rock dusts, composting and, **21, 72, 104**

S
Sandy soil, **84–85**
   effect of humus on, **86**
Sawdust, as compost material, **124–25**
Seaweed, as compost material, **125**
Sewage sludge, as compost material, **126**
Sheep manure, as compost material, **121**
Sheet composting, **20–21**
   rock dusts for, **21**
Side-dressing, using compost as, **73**
Snow fencing pen
   composting in, **45**
   drawbacks of, **45**
Soil
   acid, **95**
   adjusting pH of, **96–98**
   alkaline, **95**
   as compost material, **127**
   neutralizing toxins in, **94**
   structure of, **84–89**
      clay, **84–85**
      loam, **84–85**
      sandy, **84–85**
Spanish moss, as compost material, **127**
Stable, as compost material source, **101**

Steel drums, as compost frames, **60–62**
Stout, Ruth, on permanent mulching, **23–24**
Straw, as compost material, **127**
Sugar wastes, as compost material, **127–28**
Synthetic fertilizer, **93**
    effect on soil and, **89**

Tobacco, as compost material, **129–30**
Trenching compost method, **16–19**

U
Urine, human, as compost material, **121**

T
Tanbark, as compost material, **128**
Tankage, as compost material, **128**
Tea grounds, as compost material, **128**
Temperature, compost pile, and measuring of, **28**
Thermophilic bacteria, **29**
Three-compartment block bin, composting in, **53–56**

W
Water hyacinth, as compost material, **129**
Weeds, as compost material, **129**
Wire pen, composting in, **43–45**
Wood ashes, as compost material, **129–30**
Wood bin, composting in, **56–57**
Wood chips, as compost material, **130**
Wood pallet pen, composting in, **46–47**
Wool wastes, as compost material, **130**